# PALACE

By the same author

*Happy and Glorious:*
For the Queen's Silver Jubilee, 1977

*The Queen's Children*

*The Royal Family in the 20th Century*

*Prince Andrew*

*Express '56:*
A year in the life of a Beaverbrook journalist

*The Stalag Men:*
A personal account of life in Hitler's Reich
As an Other Rank P.O.W.

*The Day of Reckoning:*
Monday, 20th May, 1940

# Donald Edgar

# PALACE

A fascinating behind-the-scenes look
at how Buckingham Palace really works

W.H. ALLEN · LONDON
*A Howard & Wyndham Company*

Typeset by Phoenix Photosetting, Chatham
Printed and bound in Great Britain by
Mackays of Chatham Ltd, Kent
for the Publishers, W.H. Allen & Co. Ltd,
44 Hill Street, London W1X 8LB

ISBN 0 491 03401 6

*Endpapers:* This view of the Palace from the south east, engraved by G. Walker in 1852, shows the east front built by Blore in 1847.

To Rosalie
Again

# Contents

'You cannot make a cheap Palace'
*Emerson, Journal, 1857*

# Introduction

W HEN THE Queen stands on the famous front balcony of Buckingham Palace, she is in a quite literal sense at the centre of much of her life as a person and her duties as sovereign. Around her stretches a unique scene set in nearly 800 acres of splendid royal parkland in the middle of one of the most populous cities in the world. Perhaps only the English could have created such a wildly eccentric paradox!

To the left, beyond Green Park, behind the vaguely Mediterranean roofs of the Dorchester Hotel in Park Lane lies Bruton Street where she was born at No. 21 on 21 April 1926. Somewhat nearer, at 145 Piccadilly (no longer existing), not far from Apsley House, the town-house of the Dukes of Wellington, was the large mansion where she grew up with her parents, the then Duke and Duchess of York.

Directly in front of the balcony is the great processional way of the Mall leading from the Victoria Memorial to Admiralty Arch and the entrance to Trafalgar Square, dominated by Nelson's Column. Along that Mall the Queen has ridden many times in state since in May 1937 as a girl of eleven, wearing as Princess Elizabeth of York a train of purple velvet and a gold coronet, she attended the coronation of her father, George VI. He had by a vagary of fate succeeded to the throne on the abdication of his elder brother, Edward VIII, who after his marriage to Mrs Simpson lived out his years of exile as the Duke of Windsor.

For the young Elizabeth the war years of 1939–45, were spent in safety from air bombing at Windsor Castle. Then came the happy return to Buckingham Palace where she stood on this balcony on VE Day with her father, mother and sister, Margaret, and experienced for the first time as an adult the sight of great crowds of loyal subjects who had come at a moment of national rejoicing to be at one with the Royal Family.

Two and a half years later, on 20 November 1947, she drove from the forecourt below for her marriage to Prince Philip in Westminster Abbey. The occasion was for the nation the first touch of pageantry seen for many drab and dangerous years. The coach had been refurbished, so had the liveries of the footmen. An escort of Household Cavalry rode alongside with waving plumes and glittering cuirasses. The Guards were back in ceremonial red tunics and bearskins. People could feel life was picking up again. For her it was a bridal day of joy beginning a life's partnership with the handsome, able man she had fallen in love with during the war when she was a girl.

After the honeymoon she and Philip lived for a time with her parents in the Palace and her first child, Prince Charles, was born here on Sunday evening, 14 November 1948. He was baptised in the magnificent, blue-columned Music Room overlooking the gardens by the then Archbishop of Canterbury, Dr (later Lord) Fisher. The Palace chapel in which she herself had been christened by the then Archbishop of York, had been damaged beyond repair by a German bomb.

The next year, 1949, she and Philip moved into Clarence House, a few hundred yards up the Mall on the left. Princess Anne was born there on 15 August 1950, but christened, like her brother, in the Music Room of the Palace.*

There were a few idyllic years for Elizabeth in Clarence House with sunlit visits to Malta where Prince Philip was serving in what was (how nostalgic the phrase sounds!) the British Mediterranean Fleet.

Her father, George VI, whose health had never been good, died on 6 February 1952 whilst she and Philip were in East Africa at the beginning of a world tour. She flew back to take up her duties as Queen at the age of twenty-five.

It was her mother who moved to Clarence House and in time picked up the threads of life with resilient courage and as Queen Mother became even more beloved. For her daughter the Queen, reigning in her own right, there opened a new world of great responsibilities matched by great privileges. Amongst them was Buckingham Palace, extending on all sides round the balcony with over 600 rooms, from the overpoweringly ornate suites of State Rooms to simple attic bedrooms for the housemaids. In the Palace, around 350 men and women would work to create the framework in

---

*Both Prince Andrew (b. 19 February 1960) and Prince Edward (b. 10 March 1964) were born in Buckingham Palace and both christened in the Music Room.

which her political, ceremonial, financial and social life would be organised with meticulous care.

Beyond the balcony across St James's Park can be seen Big Ben and the Victoria Tower, the two landmarks of the House of Commons and the House of Lords, housed in what is the Queen's Palace of Westminster. She is a constitutional monarch, obliged to accept the decisions of the government of the day, but she is the sovereign and every year in the autumn drives in state along the Mall to the Palace of Westminster. From her throne there, encrowned, she reads to the Lords and Commons the speech presented to her by her Lord Chancellor setting out her Government's programme for the following year.

Along the skyline of Whitehall are the Italianate palazzi built by Palmerston in the nineteenth century to house the Home Office, the Foreign Office, the Treasury – all controlled by one of her Majesty's Ministers. There, hidden by the foliage of trees in summer, is Downing Street where at No. 10 the Prime Minister resides. Every Tuesday, when Parliament is sitting and the Queen is in residence, her Prime Minister has an audience in Buckingham Palace, and reports on the state of the nation. She also listens to the Queen's comments and, in times of crisis, to her warnings.

A little to the right of the Houses of Parliament are the noble towers of Westminster Abbey, and for the Queen there was from the time of her accession an appointment with destiny there – her coronation. Nearly 900 years before, on Christmas Day 1066, William of Normandy confirmed his conquest of the Kingdom earlier that year by receiving the crown there. Since then, every sovereign has been crowned in the Abbey except for Edward V, murdered as a boy in the Tower by his uncle, Richard III, and Edward VIII, who abdicated in December 1936 before his coronation.

The day of the coronation of Elizabeth II was Tuesday, 2 June 1953. She prepared herself for the occasion not just with the new gowns but by thought and prayer, for she is a sincere Christian and appreciates that since the Reformation the sovereign has been supreme Governor of the Church of England. She drove out on the morning through the quadrangle in the fantastic eighteenth-century golden State coach with its seven panels painted by Cipriani, its tritons and palm-trees, surmounted by the Imperial Crown, the Sceptre and Sword of State. After the long, exhausting, but fulfilling ceremony she drove back in the afternoon through vast crowds braving the rain. There were repeated appearances here on the balcony and in a broadcast from the Palace she said in a voice of limpid sincerity:

'I have behind me, not only the splendid traditions and annals of more than one thousand years, but the living strength and majesty of the Commonwealth and Empire, of societies old and new, of lands and races differing in history and origin, but all, by God's will, united in spirit and aim.'

Since that day thirty years ago the Empire has almost entirely disappeared, but the Commonwealth is there and the Queen looks upon her work of preserving and fostering it as one of her principal achievements. The leaders of the countries have often been to Buckingham Palace singly and in groups for informal talks or for great ceremonial receptions and banquets. There on the left of the Mall the Commonwealth has its headquarters in Marlborough House, built for John Churchill, the great Duke of Marlborough, but later a very grand royal residence. During the long reign of Victoria the Prince of Wales (later Edward VII) made it a centre of London social life, not without a certain vulgar raffishness which made his mother shake her head over 'the Marlborough set'.

When Edward succeeded to the throne his eldest son, George, took over Marlborough House with his wife, Mary. She was very happy there and regretted having to leave when her husband became King as George V in 1910 and she had to move to Buckingham Palace. She soon became, however, by virtue of her knowledge and taste, one of the lasting influences on its interior.

When George V died in January 1936 she moved back to Marlborough House, and died there at the age of eighty-five just before the coronation of her granddaughter, Elizabeth II. Close links had grown up between the two, and Queen Mary rejoiced to see her happily married and to live to see her great-grandchildren, Charles and Anne.

Between Clarence House and Marlborough House lies St James's Palace, built by Henry VIII. Within its walls, burned down and then rebuilt, many of the Queen's ancestors, Tudor, Stuart and Hanoverian, were born, christened, married, reigned and died.

*Previous page:* This statue in honour of their grandmother was unveiled in 1911 by King George V in the presence of his cousin, Emperor Wilhelm of Germany.

Kaiser Wilhelm, who three years later was to lead his country into the 1914–18 war, had a strange affection for England. This was to be his last visit.

Though the court was finally transferred to Buckingham Palace in Victoria's reign, a new sovereign is still proclaimed by the heralds from the balcony overlooking the courtyard in St James's Palace to the sound of trumpets.

The most poignant memory of St James's Palace for a British sovereign is that of Charles I, who spent the last night of his life there. On the morning of 30 January 1649 he was escorted in solemn procession to the Banqueting Hall of Whitehall Palace for execution.

That noble Inigo Jones building still stands with its glorious Rubens ceiling commissioned by Charles in honour of his father, James I, the first Stuart King of England.

Charles stepped from a first floor window to the scaffold and died with dignity under the axe as the drums beat loudly and drowned the cries of pity and horror from the crowd.

This event is part of the Queen's consciousness for out of the bloody seventeenth-century struggle between King and Parliament grew finally the establishment of a constitutional monarchy which came to fruition, more by luck than judgment, when her ancestor George of Hanover inherited the British crown in 1714 by virtue of his Stuart blood on the female side.

Past St James's Palace and a few yards to the right is the extensive, gravelled Horse Guards Parade where daily the Household Cavalry mount a guard and where on her official birthday (11 June) the Queen rides in uniform to the Trooping of the Colour ceremony mounted in her honour by the Brigade of Guards. The Queen is by her position head of all the Armed Services, but there is a specially close link between the sovereign and the Household Troops. In peacetime their duties are mainly ceremonial, but in war they have earned a reputation of fearless gallantry.

From the balcony the Queen can see on the right by the Palace the Guards' Wellington barracks in Birdcage Walk, and just beyond the rebuilt Guards chapel which was destroyed during the war when it was unfortunately crowded with worshippers, many of whom were killed.

From the balcony the barracks of the Household Cavalry cannot be seen, but they are not far away round the corner in Knightsbridge, housed and stabled in new buildings designed by Sir Basil Spence with a lofty tower which has ever since aroused controversy as a useless folly. The site of the barracks is on the southern fringe of Hyde Park and leads past the Albert Hall and the Albert Memorial (named after Queen Victoria's consort) to Kensington Palace.

In the opinion of many this is the most elegant of the royal palaces.

It was built by Wren in the 1690s for William and Mary, who came over from Holland in 1688 to reign jointly after her father James II, the last Stuart King, had fled to France to escape the wrath of a people angered by his increasing tyranny and Catholic bigotry.

The palace has long been used to provide apartments for the Royal Family. The Prince and Princess of Wales now live there. Princess Margaret has been there for many years. There is no doubt, however, as to who was the most illustrious member of the Royal Family to live there. One of the most moving moments in the history of the British monarchy is that dawn of Tuesday, 20 June 1837 when the Archbishop of Canterbury and the Lord Chamberlain arrived at Kensington Palace and demanded to see Princess Victoria. After an inordinate delay caused by servants reluctant to wake her at 5 a.m., she came down with a shawl round her dressing-gown, her fair hair on her shoulders and slippers on her feet. The two great dignitaries then knelt and kissed her hand as Queen of England. Her uncle, William IV, had died during the night without legitimate issue.

Victoria had celebrated her eighteenth birthday less than a month before on 24 May. She soon showed her mettle and determination to leave behind her the humiliation of having a bed in the room of her mother, the Duchess of Kent, in Kensington Palace. Within a week she was ordering from Mr Snell of Albemarle Street, curtains, hangings, coverings and carpets for Buckingham Palace. For when she came to the throne it was just about ready for occupation, twelve years after her other uncle, George IV (the former Prince Regent) had started planning the rebuilding of what had been known before as 'The Queen's House' or 'Buckingham House'. He had not lived long enough to see the Palace completed, nor had his younger brother, William IV, who succeeded in 1830.

Three weeks and two days after her accession, Victoria moved into her own Buckingham Palace. There she could be Queen and her own mistress after all the constraints and financial stringencies of her life in Kensington Palace.

And although she virtually abandoned Buckingham Palace after the death of Prince Albert in 1861, her reign left its mark. The balcony itself is part of the eastern façade built 1847–50 which completely ruined the original concept of the Palace.

As Queen Elizabeth II looks down from the balcony, just in front of the forecourt lies the huge Victoria Memorial on its island site. It was unveiled by George V in 1911 and among the guests was the Kaiser, Victoria's grandson, who led the Germans in the 1914–18 war which destroyed the fabric of European civilisation for all time.

One of the most moving moments in the history of the British monarchy
. . . when the Archbishop of Canterbury and the Lord Chamberlain con-
veyed the news of the King's death to Princess Victoria, and then knelt
and kissed her hand as Queen of England.

To the right of the balcony, hidden by the façade and other buildings, lies Victoria Station, named after the Queen, for it was built in the great days of railway expansion in which Britain led the world. Now when the Queen greets the monarchs and presidents of the world who come on State visits they usually arrive by train (after a flight to Gatwick) at the same Victoria Station.

Memories of scenes from the balcony are mainly happy. There was, however, an exception. Between the Palace and St James's a dangerous attempt was made on 20 March 1974 to kidnap Princess Anne when she was returning in the early evening along the Mall with her husband, Captain Mark Phillips, after a film show. Ian Ball, then twenty-six years old, had conceived a daring plan to raise a great ransom and was ruthless in its execution. He drove his car in front of the royal Austin Princess which was forced to halt. In the ensuing affray the Princess's detective was shot three times. The chauffeur and a nearby policeman were also shot before help arrived. At one moment it seemed that Ball in desperation would shoot Anne. At the time the Queen and Prince Philip were far away in the East visiting Indonesia. So even a note of dangerous drama is not missing as the Queen looks round from that balcony which has played such an essential part in her life.

The scene covers an area which is almost a royal enclave, whose splendid buildings with their towers and spires recount stirring chapters of British history. It also has, however, an important significance for today. Buckingham Palace not only stands there in the middle of London at the centre of much of British life. It has become the symbol of British monarchy, both here and abroad.

The British monarchy, constitutional as it is, cannot be compared with the constitutional monarchies of say, Scandinavia, or even Holland. In the course of the centuries the British monarchy has become inextricably embedded in the national life in countless ways from Church, Parliament, Government, Civil Service, Armed Forces, the Law to the patronage of countless institutions and societies. The ramifications spread through nearly every activity so it is not fanciful to feel that if the monarchy fell, so would Britain.

Buckingham Palace is the centre of all this organised royal participation, the indispensable power-house of the monarchy. Yet, such is the irony of life, few of the Royal Family have ever liked the Palace. Many have actively disliked it. Some, like Edward VII and VIII have gone further and called it, 'a Mausoleum' and 'a Sepulchre'.

In their time George V and VI preferred the rôles of 'Laird of Balmoral' or 'Squire of Sandringham'.

Queen Elizabeth II has left no doubt where her loyalties lie. Giving her 1982 Christmas broadcast from Windsor Castle, she said with some emphasis, 'This is my home', and went on to talk of its foundation as a military fort by William the Conqueror.

You could say of Buckingham Palace that it is 'the Palace they love to hate'.

# The Early
# Tenants

*B*UCKINGHAM PALACE stands on Church land seized by the Crown when the monasteries were dissolved in the sixteenth century by the ruthless Thomas Cromwell for Henry VIII. There is nothing unusual in this background, for a fifth of the land of the Kingdom was appropriated in this manner in what was the greatest land grab since the Norman Conquest 500 years earlier.

Henry VIII was greatly enriched in the process; so were favoured supporters of the Tudor monarchy such as the Russells, Cavendishes and Fitzwilliams who became great landowners, and in time joined the aristocracy which was indeed in need of fresh blood after the butchery of the Wars of the Roses had cut down the ranks of the old Norman families on whichever side they had fought.

Where St James's Palace now stands was a leper hospital lying in unfrequented fields. It was dedicated by the religious order which ran it to St James the Less. Henry kept the saint's name when he demolished the hospital and built the Palace, as much for Anne Boleyn as for himself. He later drained and laid out some of the surrounding fields as a pleasure garden, the beginning of St James's Park.

At the western boundary of the land lay a marshy area often flooded by the waters of two streams, the West Bourne and Tyburn. For a long time it remained wasteland, the haunt of wildfowl, but eventually plots were given away or sold by the Crown and gradually were enclosed and drained. By the time of James I there were no more than four acres left in royal hands.

It was a time when English landowners were planting gardens of imported mulberry trees in the hope of founding a native silk industry. James was so taken with this development that in 1609 he financed a Mulberry Garden on these remaining four acres which were roughly where the Palace forecourt is today. The scheme failed, as did the others in England, although one in Chelsea on the old site of Sir Thomas More's estate by the Thames is said to have produced silk enough for coronation robes.

King James's Mulberry Gardens venture may have failed commercially, but it began the royal connection with those former marshy acres of wasteland which culminated in the building of Buckingham Palace on the site. In and around the Mulberry Gardens three noblemen in the seventeenth and early eighteenth centuries extended their land holdings and each in turn built a mansion of increasing size which was named after him – Goring House, Arlington House and Buckingham House.

They all lived dangerously in those decades of civil war, religious persecution and revolution. They were all close to the throne and devoted to the House of Stuart, even when it fell. If their shadows still wander by the lake in the gardens of Buckingham Palace, they would have adventurous stories to tell.

## GORING HOUSE

George Goring (1583?–1663), later Lord Goring and Earl of Norwich, laid the foundations of his fortune as a buffoon and prankster at the court of James I, but was soon to show more serious qualities. He became a gentleman in the court of Prince Henry – the strong, able eldest son of James who died, probably of typhoid, at the age of eighteen thereby opening the succession to his younger brother, the weak, sickly boy who became Charles I.

Goring was then entrusted with the negotiations in Paris for the marriage of Charles to the Princess Henrietta Maria of France. The fruitful outcome made Goring's career. He was created a peer, given the monopolies on tobacco and taverns which produced an almost princely income and when Henrietta Maria became Queen he was appointed her Vice-Chamberlain and Master of Horse. These royal favours enabled him to build Goring House alongside the Mulberry Gardens. It was a fine, gabled mansion with a Fountain Garden, Terrace Walk and a Mount set with trees. He lived there in courtly, extravagant style with a train of hangers-on.

At the outbreak of the Civil War between Charles and Parliament he exclaimed, 'Had I millions of crowns or scores of sons the King should have them all.' Goring certainly did lose nearly all his crowns in the war. He accompanied the Queen to Holland in 1642 to raise money for the cause and returned to become a courageous, if not very skilful commander. His two sons, another George, and Henry, charged together at the second battle of Newbury. George seemed to be an archetype of the Cavalier of history – profligate, prodigal, brilliant – and proved himself one of the ablest of Charles's commanders. As General of the Horse he aroused the jealousy of the great cavalry leader, Prince Rupert, the King's nephew.*

Goring was imprisoned on the defeat of the royalist armies, tried, sentenced to death and escaped his fate only by intervention of a man to whom he had done a chance favour in the past. He went into exile and his house was used for a time to accommodate a French Embassy and then as a barracks for Commonwealth troops when it suffered inevitable damage.

In and around the Mulberry Garden at this time, however, flourished a place of resort and refreshment for gallants and their ladies 'of the best quality', as Evelyn, a diarist of the *haut ton*, records. It was a surprising development since the puritan régime was closing down most places of entertainment including Spring Gardens, at the bottom of Whitehall, where Charles I had played on the bowling-green and the fashionable world had gathered.

At the Restoration in 1660 Goring returned to England, but it was for him a different landscape. His princely income had gone; Goring House was occupied by an enterprising caterer by the name of O'Neale who supplied the clientèle in the Gardens. Goring's title to the property was tenuous. He had taken out large mortgages on the property which had fallen in over the years. There were other claimants; chicanery and fraud by lawyers added to the confusion.

He never recovered house or land. Nor did his successors. He was, however, more fortunate than many of the ruined Cavaliers. Charles II gave him a handsome pension and the earldom so that the last few years of the stalwart Goring were not humiliating.

Goring House never became part of the Mulberry Garden 'leisure complex' as it would be described today. Pepys, a more bourgeois diarist than Evelyn, wrote:

'. . . walked over the Park to Mulberry Garden, where I never was before; and find it a very silly place, worse than Spring Garden, and but little company, and those a rascally, whoring, roguing sort of

---

*Clarendon, the historian who was a participant in all these events has a different story. He writes that this Goring played a double game: 'of all his qualifications, dissimulation was his masterpiece'. He would 'without hesitation, have broken any trust, or done any act of treachery, to have satisfied an ordinary passion or appetite; and, in truth, wanted nothing but industry (for he had wit, and courage, and understanding, and ambition, uncontrolled by any fear of God or man) to have been as eminent and successful in the highest attempt in wickedness of any man in the age he lived in, or before.'
A devastating judgment on the Cavalier paladin!

people, only a wilderness here, that is somewhat pretty, but rude. Did not stay to drink, but walked an hour, and so away to Charing Cross.'

So much for the future stately grounds of Buckingham Palace!

## ARLINGTON HOUSE

Grandeur was soon to return, however, on a new high level. In 1665, Henry Bennet (1618–1685), later Earl of Arlington, scholar, diplomat and a member of the notorious 'Cabal' (an embryonic Cabinet), Lord Chamberlain and an intimate of both Charles II and James II – in fact one of the Jacobean grandees – came to live in Goring House. In 1672 he was granted a ninety-nine-year lease by the Crown.

He completely redecorated the mansion, furnished it splendidly, acquired paintings from his agents abroad and entertained on a lavish scale. During his years abroad as a diplomat, working for the exiled Charles and James, he had married Isabella van Beverweert, daughter of Louis of Nassau, a princely family. Henry Bennet had arrived!

He possessed to a consummate degree the art of dissembling which was an essential quality for survival in those days. He knew that Charles II was a secret Roman Catholic and pensioner of Louis XIV. He knew that James was a fervent Roman Catholic determined to bring back the faith to England. But then he was also a secret Roman Catholic himself. These allegiances seem of little import now. In those days they were perilous.

The year 1674 was a difficult one for Arlington. Goring House burned down and he was impeached by Parliament for popery, embezzlement and betrayal of trust. But he surmounted his troubles. By his cunning wits he extricated himself from the impeachment charges and was wealthy enough to rebuild Goring House grandly and changed its name to Arlington House. He bought some adjoining land from the Grosvenor estate so that in time his grounds comprised: 'The Oval Court and Flower Garden, the Terrace Walk, the Dwarf Tree Garden, the Wilderness, the Grove and Bowling Green, the very extensive Orange Houses with the Bagnio, Bathing Cisterns and the like.' There was stabling for forty or more horses, including a dozen hunters. Indoors there was a suite of fine reception rooms, a well-appointed chapel and 'a long gallery of nine sash windows towards (St James's) Park'.

Arlington, to a certain extent, outlived his times and his arrogant, patronising manner annoyed the younger generation of courtiers. Having performed his duties as Lord Chamberlain at the coronation of James II he died a man of title and property with an estate at Euston in Suffolk as well as Arlington House. This he bequeathed to his only child, Isabella, who at an early age had married Henry Fitzroy, a son of Charles II by Barbara Villiers, later Lady Castlemaine and Duchess of Cleveland.

Fitzroy, created Duke of Grafton in 1675, was killed in 1690 leading an impetuous attack at the siege of Cork. He left a son only seven years old. His trustees let Arlington House, first to the Duke of Devonshire and then in 1698 to John Sheffield, Earl of Mulgrave. In 1702 the property was sold to Sheffield and confirmed in 1704 when the young Duke of Grafton came of age.

By this time Sheffield had been created Duke of Buckingham and that title is the origin of the name the Palace bears today.

## BUCKINGHAM HOUSE

John Sheffield (1648–1721) is a very attractive character – soldier, sailor, poet, patron of literature, courtier, adventurous lover and, for those days, amazingly loyal. His portrait after a painting by Sir Godfrey Kneller hangs in the National Portrait Gallery and shows a handsome, proud man, elegant in his fitted armour with a lace jabot at his neck, his fine hands posed with studied negligence in the Van Dyck style.

He was born an aristocrat, inheriting the title of Earl of Mulgrave. At the age of eighteen he served as a volunteer with Prince Rupert, who had now successfully changed his role from land to sea and led a fleet against the Dutch. Sheffield developed into an able sea captain and later, on land, his courageous leadership brought him the colonelcy of a Regiment of Foot. At court, his charm and ability made him a favourite of both Charles II and the future James II. In 1674 at the age of twenty-six he was created a Knight of the Garter and was soon enjoying the fruits of profitable offices.

In his early thirties Sheffield, basking in royal favour, raised his bold eyes to the seventeen-year-old Princess Anne, the younger daughter of James II by Anne Hyde. When she became Queen in 1702, twenty years later, she showed in truly royal fashion that the attentions of Sheffield had not been unwelcome. At the time, however, the courtship was disastrous for Sheffield. Charles II, her uncle, angered at his presumption, stripped him of his places and banished him from court.

In a year or two, however, he was back in favour, and when James II succeeded his brother in 1685 he became Lord Chamberlain and an intimate adviser. This leads to the supposition that he was another secret Roman Catholic.

Sheffield's close links with James were sealed by a blood relation when he married his third wife, Catherine Darnley, the King's illegitimate daughter by Catherine Sedley, Countess of Dorchester. In an oil painting at Southill Park,* Sheffield's Catherine looks a strong-minded woman, but not without romantic good looks. So, as he could not have Anne, he had married her half-sister, Catherine.

In 1688, William of Orange, who was married to Mary, James's other daughter by Anne Hyde, was invited over to England by the Protestant Whig lords to lead the revolution against James II, whose rule had degenerated into a tyranny designed to restore the Roman Catholic Church. James found himself abandoned by nearly everyone, including those to whom he had shown great favour.

These were years when many leading Englishmen displayed a cynical ingratitude that made Europe sneer at their treachery, but Sheffield was among the few who remained loyal. He stayed with James until the King left England. What is more, when William and Mary came to the throne, he did not go over to them, but was one of the leaders of the Tory opposition. He survived, but once more, lost all his offices.

In 1694 Queen Mary died, followed by William in 1702. Anne, the last Stuart monarch, came to the throne and the sun shone warmly again for faithful Sheffield. He was given office and a handsome pension, created Marquess of Normanby and then Duke of Buckingham. Now in such a high position he decided to pull down Arlington House, round off the property with a slice of Crown land to which the Queen, a little reluctantly at first, agreed, and then build with splendour what was virtually a medium-sized palace. The grounds were laid out with grandeur by the royal gardener in the formal elegance fashionable at the time.

The House was approached through a fine iron gateway, a spacious forecourt with a capacious fountain in the centre decorated with statues of Neptune and the Triton. The frieze over the House was decorated with Latin inscriptions in bold gold lettering: '*SIC*

---

*A fine early Georgian mansion near Ampthill in Bedfordshire. It has for generations belonged to the Whitbread family, local benefactors.

*SITU LAETANTUR LARES'* (The Household Gods delight in such a situation): *'RUS IN URBE'* (Country within the City).

Sheffield lived with his Duchess in princely style, held his own levée, wrote poetry and prose, was a friend of Pope, a munificent patron of Dryden and thoroughly enjoyed life. He read, listened to the nightingales in his gardens and strolled through his grand apartments decorated by Italian artists (of which there are water-colours and prints).

They were happy years, but then Queen Anne died in 1714 and was succeeded by George I, the first of the Hanovers. Once more Sheffield lost all his lucrative posts, but he seems to have foreseen this probable change of fortune and had put funds aside. Certainly he still lived in great style and once more survived accusations, probably correct, that Buckingham House was a centre of Jacobite plotting.

The Duke died in 1721, lay in state like a prince and was then carried to Westminster Abbey and buried in the Henry VII Chapel. He left the House and gardens to his Duchess for her life, providing she did not marry again. She did not, and lived on in semi-royal state at Buckingham House dressed in crimson velvet and ermine, attended by ladies-in-waiting and a large retinue of servants. Every year on the anniversary of the execution of her grandfather, King Charles I, she wore robes of deepest mourning and ensured her household dressed in black.

Two years after the death of the Duke, the Prince and Princess of Wales (the future King George II and his Queen) tried to lease or buy Buckingham House from the Duchess. She deliberately asked an extravagant price and the deal fell through. Her son by Sheffield, Edmund, the second Duke of Buckingham, died unmarried in Rome at the age of twenty in 1735 and the title became extinct. In 1742 the indomitable Duchess died worrying about the delivery of her funeral canopy and the fulfilment of her orders that her ladies should not sit in her presence until she was pronounced dead.

The property then passed to Charles Herbert, an illegitimate son of John Sheffield. He took his father's name and was created a baronet in 1755. He discovered in time that there were many flaws in his father's title to the land and in 1761, mindful that the lease had not many years to run, was receptive to generous offers from the Crown. The purchase was made and Sheffield got a good price. Thus in 1762 George III, a year after his coronation and marriage to Charlotte of Mecklenburg-Strelitz, acquired Buckingham House and its grounds. The ostensible motive was to provide a Dower House for the Queen.

From now on the role to be played was indisputably, legally and legitimately royal. It was 'The Queen's House'.

The Sheffield link with the Royal Family was romantically revived more than two centuries later in 1974. The Prince of Wales, then twenty-six, was captivated by Davina Sheffield, three years younger, whom he had first met at a dinner-party given by Lady Jane Wellesley, the daughter of the Duke of Wellington. At that time Lady Jane was considered a very likely bride for Charles. Davina is a direct descendant of the baronet who had sold Buckingham House to George III. Her family is also related to Mrs Keppel, the last and most lasting of Edward VII's mistresses. When the King lay dying in Buckingham Palace* Queen Alexandra agreed to a suggestion that Alice Keppel should be allowed to say farewell. When Mrs Keppel arrived, the Queen took her by the hand and led her to the bedside.

Davina Sheffield and her sister, Laura, led the 'debby' life of the times in the Chelsea-Fulham Road area. They ran a craft shop on Chelsea Green selling Irish cottage industry products, basketwork and flowerpots. That year Charles was always in Davina's company. She was invited to Balmoral by the Queen. She went on holiday with Charles to a small fishing village on the south-west coast. The press began to talk of marriage.

Charles was at that time serving in the Navy and went back to duty. At about that time, a former boyfriend of Davina ungallantly talked to the press about his friendship with her in some detail and probably wrecked any marriage prospects for good and all. The next year Davina broke away from the Chelsea set and went to Saigon where the Vietnam war was nearing a disastrous end for the USA. She worked in a refugee orphanage for some time with courageous zeal. When she returned in the summer of 1975 Charles renewed the friendship. She was at Windsor several times watching him play polo and sat in the royal box with the Queen and Philip. The marriage rumours started up again, but that season proved to be Davina's swan-song.

It is an irony of history that at the court of Charles II John Sheffield had courted Princess Anne and for a time suffered for it. Now in the 1970s Davina Sheffield had been courted by the Prince of Wales. This time it was the woman who suffered.

---

*King Edward VII has been the only monarch to die in Buckingham Palace. Queen Victoria died at Osborne on the Isle of Wight and George V and his son, George VI, at Sandringham in Norfolk.

## THE QUEEN'S HOUSE

The eighteen-year-old Queen Charlotte asked her husband King George III to delay the celebrations of his twenty-fourth birthday on 4 June 1762 for two days as she was preparing a surprise for the house-warming at the Queen's House. The King waited at St James's Palace along the road until the evening of the sixth. When he arrived the Queen took him up to a first-floor apartment overlooking the gardens. The shutters were closed. Then she told the awaiting servants to pull them aside. In front of George lay a splendid scene. A temple and bridge had been erected, as if by magic, and were illuminated by 4000 glass lamps. From behind, their light illuminated a giant transparency representing the King giving peace to all parts of the globe, 'at His Majesty's feet Envy, Malice and Detraction were seen falling headlong'. Simultaneously a band (the Queen had her own, dressed in uniforms of scarlet and gold) struck up a selection of the King's favourite airs.

It is pleasant, even now, to recall the welcome given to the young King by his bride from the little German state of Mecklenburg-Strelitz who had come over a year before at the age of seventeen to be married in the chapel of St James's Palace. Charlotte was not beautiful or witty, but she gave herself in entirety to be an intelligent, helpful Queen and in long years of sorrow comforted a beloved husband stricken by mental illness.

That, however, was fortunately all hidden in time. The young Queen was delighted with her new home. It was her own, a Dower House given to her by the King. As it turned out, however, the Queen's House became the home of the Royal Family in London whilst the formal state ceremonies were performed at St James's Palace.

George and Charlotte really did make the House their home. Their eldest son, the future Prince Regent and George IV, was born at St James's, but at the Queen's House, she bore fourteen more children, of whom only two died in childbirth. Like her husband, who had spent his youth surrounded by the gardens of Kew, Charlotte loved flowers, and her House was always filled with them. She also ensured that the rooms were made comfortably warm by constantly tended fires. That was an achievement no one ever seems to have been able to match in the Buckingham Palace that was to rise around the House.

George did make changes in and around the House. All the panache of Sheffield's design was eliminated with a few, but quite devastating alterations. The great ornamental gate, the elaborate fountain and the enlivening sweep of the forecourt were swept away. So were the elegant open arcades of the wings. The gesticulating neo-classical statues decorating the line of the roof, which gave such a sense of excitement, were replaced by batteries of chimneys. In the quest for privacy (how often that desire was to be expressed by the Royal Family!) George erected a dull, uniform fence of iron railings along the entire front of the House so that entrance could be made only round the corners to the left and right.

It is quite remarkable to compare views of Buckingham House and the Queen's House. The first looks elegant and interesting; the second, mediocre and institutional. It is a misfortune that this negative aspect of Georgian style should have marked the King's influence on the exterior of the Queen's House for he made admirable contributions inside.

In those happy early years in the House, George and Charlotte created a cultured ambiance which has left its influence on Buckingham Palace (and, perhaps, Windsor Castle). The King and Queen were fortunate to live at a propitious time, and have ample funds, but they made excellent use of their opportunities. George was a great collector of books (67,000 volumes) and to house them in dignity he had the noble Octagonal Library built on the south side of the House. In time, more rooms were added and another storey was built in 1774 for the King's Marine Gallery where he kept his models of ships and harbours. It was in the Octagonal Library that the famous conversation took place in 1767 between the King and Dr Johnson, who had the freedom, with a few other scholars, to read

*Above:* This fine engraving by Sutton Nichols published by John Bowles, shows Buckingham House in St James's Park as it looked in 1754. Notice the great ornamental gate and fountain of John Sheffield's house. Eight years later in 1762, George III acquired the house and grounds and subsequently swept away the gate and fountain and the gesticulating statues lining the roof.

*Below:* Buckingham House, sometimes called The Queen's House, after George III had made his changes to Sheffield's design. This engraving by J. Miller was made in 1796.

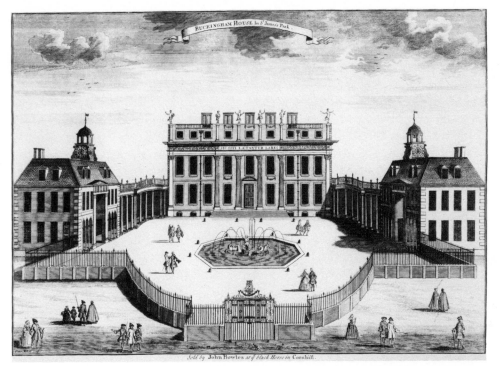

BUCKINGHAM HOUSE In S.t James's Park.

SIC SITI LÆTANTUR LARES

London

Sold by John Bowles at y.e black Horse in Cornhill.

37

there. Boswell reports the meeting as told to him in detail by Johnson. When the King left, Johnson remarked to the librarian: 'Sir, they may talk of the King as they will; but he is the finest gentleman I have ever seen.'*

The King's library was later given in part to the British Museum by his son, George IV, where the gift is proudly entitled 'The King's Library'. Another part went to Windsor Castle to form a library.

George III had scientific curiosity at a time when a technological revolution was about to break in England and make it the workshop of the world. He spent lavishly, but wisely, on a collection of splendid, elaborate timepieces by the great English clockmakers of the day. With the addition of the two magnificent clocks and a barometer made by Tompion for William and Mary, and their successor Queen Anne, George had a great collection and it is today one of the most important treasures of Buckingham Palace.

It was, however, in his first year at the Queen's House (1762) that the King made his most memorable purchase. He bought the celebrated collection of Joseph Smith, who had been British consul in Venice since 1744 and become a discriminating patron, especially of Canaletto. Apart from coins, medals, cameos and books, Smith's collection contained fifty paintings by Canaletto and 150 drawings. (The Canalettos now hang for the most part in Windsor, but there was a comprehensive exhibition in the public Queen's Gallery at Buckingham Palace that lasted from December 1980 to February 1982.) There were also many paintings by other Venetian artists, notably Zuccarelli. What would now be considered the most precious jewel in the collection was Vermeer's, 'The Music Lesson, a Lady at the Virginals with a Gentleman Listening'. Another valuable purchase was the collection of drawings belonging to Cardinal Albani of Rome which contained works of first-class quality by Domenichino, the Carracci and Poussin.

The King played a considerable part in the founding of the Royal Academy in terms of money and patronage, and both he and the Queen provided work for a number of artists. They were both

---

*This is from Boswell in his *Life of Samuel Johnson*, but in his revealing *London Journal* of 1762–63 he has less august personal reminiscences of the House and neighbourhood. He had lodgings in Downing Street and as a young Scot of noble family, enjoyed the entrée to society. But at times he preferred the common touch. He would walk across St James's Park to talk to the sentries at the Queen's House who were rewarded with a pint of beer for their conversation. Somewhat pompously he comments, 'I have great pleasure in conversing with the lower part of mankind, who have very curious ideas.'

admirers of Gainsborough. George sat for him at least seven times and commissioned the famous series of oval portraits of himself, the Queen and thirteen of their children. Zoffany was also a favoured artist and was kept busy with commissions from both the King and Queen.

Josiah Wedgwood had started his potteries in 1763 and Queen Charlotte's early patronage was of great help in establishing their fame. In 1765 Josiah wrote to his brother John: 'Pray put on the best suit of clothes you ever had in your life and take the first opportunity of going to court.' Wedgwood's famed production, 'The Queen's Ware', was named for Charlotte. She was also a patron of Matthew Boulton, the great Birmingham metal-worker, who mounted some of the Wedgwood vases in ormolu.

It was a splendid period for English cabinet-making. Charlotte placed her orders not so much with Chippendale as with Vile, Cobb and other first-class craftsmen. The Palace was enriched with their work. Indeed, there was a great deal of agreeable activity during those early years when George and Charlotte were making their home in the Queen's House. Furniture was chosen from St James's and Kensington Palaces; and the seven great Raphael cartoons, bought by Charles I in Brussels, were brought from Hampton Court where they had been hanging in a room designed by Wren for the purpose by orders of William III. (The cartoons, after moves to Windsor and Hampton Court, were loaned by Queen Victoria in 1865 to what is now the Victoria and Albert Museum. There they hang now in a magnificent gallery.)

The incomparable Van Dyck portraits commissioned by Charles I of himself, his Queen, children and relatives had been reassembled after the royal art collection of quite outstanding international importance had been largely dispersed by Oliver Cromwell's Government.*

This is how George and Charlotte spent the early years of their married life. She was nearly always pregnant, but this did not seem to disturb the pattern of their lives, surrounded by beauty, with the sound of music drifting from the rooms – perhaps Haydn, of whom

---

*Queen Elizabeth II generously loaned the greatest of these portraits to the Van Dyck Exhibition at the National Portrait Gallery in the winter of 1982–3. With loans from Paris, Leningrad and elsewhere in addition to those from public and private galleries in Britain, this was probably the most comprehensive and exciting exhibition of Van Dyck's work ever to be mounted.

Charlotte, herself a musician, was also a patron. But such idyllic scenes were not destined to last. The King, under the influence of his mother, the widowed Princess of Wales,* packed Parliament with his supporters and in time provoked rising and violent opposition. George, who had at first enjoyed considerable popularity, now found himself the object of scorn and derision.

In 1770 the government, led by his Prime Minister, Lord North, persisted in an unyielding policy towards the American colonies which led to their rebellion and Declaration of Independence on 4 July 1776.

The sunlit years of the Queen's House had, however, already been fading by then. George's mother died at Kew in 1772 and he began to spend more and more of his time there with his growing family. Perhaps he felt that in surroundings where he had spent his youth he could escape from reality and find a certain 'back to the womb' security. Kew became for a few years a centre for the Royal Family. Finding his mother's house too small George had it pulled down and began to build a riverside palace. In the meantime he resided in the modest Dutch House, which is now called Kew Palace. The King's new venture was never completed. The sons were scattered in houses on Kew Green with their tutors and servants. They had breakfast with their parents, then studied, worked on the model farms, played cricket and once a week walked in pairs behind the King and Queen along the towpath to Richmond. For a time George found solace in the peace and beauty of Kew.

When he had to attend to business in London, the ministers who reported to him in the Queen's House had little but bad news in those years. France and Spain declared war in support of the American rebels and their fleets outnumbered ours. In North America our forces blundered to final defeat and Britain was forced to conclude a humiliating peace which increased the King's unpopularity at home.

Later his cup of bitterness was filled with the dissolute extravagance of his sons as they grew up, led by the Prince of Wales. In the Queen's House there were scenes of angry quarrels which exhausted the King. There was no harmony any longer in the house, only discord.

Illness now came to plague the King. He had been troubled with

---

*George III's father, Frederick, Prince of Wales, had died in the lifetime of his father, George II.

nervous attacks as early as 1765, but now in 1788 his mental condition deteriorated seriously. By the end of the year his doctors had come to the conclusion that he would either die soon or become permanently mad. But he recovered the next year, 1789, the year which saw the beginning of the French Revolution.

There followed the terrible, uncertain years of war with Revolutionary and Napoleonic France. The King remained in reasonably good health and witnessed the turning of the tide for Britain. In 1811, however, it became necessary to appoint the Prince of Wales as Prince Regent. For nine more years the old King lived on with his hallucinations at Windsor, a desperately tragic end for a monarch who had given so much promise in those happy years when he and Charlotte were young.

Charlotte still came to London to preside over her Drawing-Rooms, seated on the throne in her Great Saloon. There is a charming, but somewhat sad water-colour drawing by Copley Fielding, 1810, showing her carriage, escorted by Horse Guards, approaching the Queen's House over the snow whilst Londoners skate on the pond in St James's Park.

George III has found a sturdy champion in his descendant, the present Prince of Wales. Charles disclosed in a television interview for the American public in 1976, the 200th anniversary of the Declaration of Independence, that George's so-called madness was, in the light of modern medical knowledge, probably a blood disease called porphyria, which gives hallucinations and depressions.

'He was a complete idealist and moralist,' Prince Charles continued. 'Either a thing was right or wrong. I am determined to clear his name. It's very unfortunate if one is misunderstood in history. I personally would hate to be misunderstood.'

## BUCKINGHAM PALACE
### QUEEN VICTORIA

When Elizabeth II entered the Palace for the first time as Queen in February 1952, she was faced by the familiar dull east façade with that narrow, gloomy, archway of the so-called grand entrance – so forbidding that it helps to explain why successive generations of the Royal Family have complained of the prison-like atmosphere within.

How different it was when Queen Victoria arrived at the Palace for the first time in July 1837! She drove through the gleaming Marble Arch into a grand open courtyard surrounded on three sides by the splendid Palace that owed its existence to that most remarkable monarch, George IV, and his architect, John Nash, who had taken on this last task at the age of seventy-three. Fortunately there is a water-colour of 1846 by Joseph Nash which shows how the Palace looked before the east façade was built. It is now in the Royal Library at Windsor Castle and must evoke feelings of anguish when examined there for it shows a Palace of romantic splendour, tempered with a certain classical restraint.

As Prince Regent and King, George was extravagant, dissolute, gluttonous, but he had a love of the arts, and an appreciation of artists that permanently enriched the cultural life of the nation – even though it often emptied the royal purse and angered successive governments which were blackmailed into refilling it.

Inside the Palace the suites of State Apartments still reflect his taste. It was he who gave the detailed instructions to his architect how they should be built and they are filled with the furniture, pictures and *objets d'art* that he painstakingly collected over many years. However much taste may have changed from time to time, succeeding monarchs have preserved these splendid rooms as their predecessor on the throne visualised them.

The exterior of the Palace was irreparably ruined by the building of the east façade between 1847 and 1850. The open courtyard that gave a sense of space was claustrophobically enclosed. Onlookers beyond the railings could no longer see the Royal Family appear in their finery on great occasions from the portico because the front door of the Palace was no longer visible. The superb Marble Arch was degraded to its present meaningless island site at the north-east corner of Hyde Park. Any sense of grandeur had been effectively eliminated and since then the image Buckingham Palace has presented to the world is the fatal east façade, designed first by

Edward Blore and then refaced in institutional style by Aston Webb in 1912 when the decaying Caen masonry was replaced with cold, formal Portland stone.

For those who attend the royal garden parties there is an opportunity to get some idea of what George IV and Nash had intended. The garden front is not one of the architect's masterpieces for it tends to ramble. It has, however, a measure of grace and elegance clad in its golden-brown Bath stone and forms an agreeable background from which the Queen and her family descend to mingle with the guests on the immaculate lawns surrounded by flowerbeds ablaze with colour. Both George and his architect would have appreciated such an occasion with the bands playing and the tents dispensing hospitality.

The architectural disaster that struck the Palace is primarily the fault of Blore, but probably the real culprit is Prince Albert. This handsome, earnest, cultured Prince of Saxe-Coburg had married Queen Victoria on 10 February 1840 in the chapel of St James's Palace. At first Victoria had excluded her husband from her constitutional work, and so he found a field for his talents in examining with German efficiency the undoubtedly lax Palace organisation. He implemented economies and controls in the manner of management consultants today. He incurred, like them, unpopularity, but he was cost-effective. His economies made it possible to build Osborne on the Isle of Wight and Balmoral on Deeside as private homes for the Royal Family.

Prince Albert was brought up in relatively modest circumstances at Rosenau Castle near Coburg, hedged in by the forests of Thuringia. His father, Duke Ernst II, lived in the style of the petty German princes of the day, grinding what money they could out of the serf-like peasants with the help of an obsequious bureaucracy and leading, to a large extent, a private life.

In England, now a dominant power, Albert found himself in an entirely different world. He was the consort of a Queen, constrained by Parliament, surrounded by a circle of often enormously rich, independently-minded aristocrats, an increasingly wealthy and politically powerful middle-class and in the background a people which had long considered itself free.

The English lords tolerated Albert, in their condescending fashion, and he had little or no contact in those early years outside this circle. He was, however, conscious of his talents and culture and reacted to his isolation by influencing the Queen, who came to hang on his every word with adoration. It was as if she and he were ruling

This engraving adapted from the painting by Winterhalter shows the Queen, Prince Albert, the Duke of Wellington and his godson, Prince Arthur, on 1 May 1851.

the sort of petty German state to which he had been born.

By 1845, five years after her marriage, Victoria had given birth to four children and it seemed likely that the number would increase (five more did, in fact, arrive). Albert explained to the Queen that in spite of the internal structural changes he had made in the Palace, their children were cramped for space. Victoria was persuaded to write to the Prime Minister, Sir Robert Peel, complaining of 'the total want of accommodation for our little family, which is fast growing up'. She also asked for a new State room larger than any the Palace possessed, new kitchens and added that the state of the exterior was a disgrace to the country. It was Albert's hand that helped to guide her pen – and those who mattered in London knew it.

These were 'the hungry forties', years of great distress and real starvation when poverty was so rife that half-farthings were issued. In 1846 *Punch* published the memorable cartoon by Sir John Leech, showing Albert standing hat in hand in front of the Palace with Victoria and the children around him. 'Good people, pray take compassion upon us,' read the caption . . . 'the sum of £150,000 will be all that will be required to make the needful alterations to our dwelling . . .'

Nevertheless, in 1847 Parliament did vote the £150,000 to build the east wing, replan the south wing, add a ballroom and new kitchen, and remove the Marble Arch. Prince Albert supervised the design of the ballroom himself and installed an organ, on which he played from time to time. Under his influence the spacious room became as much a concert hall as a ballroom.

It is difficult to be sure how much influence Albert had on Blore in the design of the new east wing. The result did realise, however, his professed desire for greater privacy. It cut the Palace off physically from the outside world as well as giving considerably more space, over fifty rooms of varying size. It was rather more than was needed for the family's nursery, children's bedrooms and schoolroom!

When Parliament made these fresh funds available it stipulated that George IV's Brighton Pavilion should be sold. Victoria raised no objection for Osborne, Albert's Italianate creation on the Isle of Wight, was being built (1845–1848) as a seaside Palace. There the Prince carried his obsession with privacy to the extent of building a separate wing for the staff so that the family could live alone as much as possible.

Brighton Pavilion proved a cornucopia of treasures – furniture, decorations, porcelain, clocks and carpets. Between 1847 and 1848, 143 van loads were taken away. There was more than enough to furnish the new wing at Buckingham Palace and the rest ended up at Windsor Castle or Kensington Palace.

Victoria's life was now led in a pattern of Albert's design. He believed in the benefits of disciplined routine. He was happiest at his desk and now he had so organised matters that his was alongside that of the Queens. Hour after hour they worked away with Albert ever ready to read the confidential papers and to give advice. It gave him power. He insisted on regular, hot meals served by efficient, silent staff. He did not like dancing, gossip or the company of men and women he considered frivolous. He liked early nights. If he was kept up late he would complain to Victoria that his health suffered (he was always complaining of headaches). He attempted to

Queen Victoria and Prince Albert taking an airing in Hyde Park.

discontinue the English habit of the men lingering over their port after the ladies had retired. In this he failed. Lord Melbourne, the Queen's Prime Minister on her accession, a sage adviser and fond admirer, told her that Albert was over-playing his hand. Though by this time Melbourne's influence over her was waning she had the sense to tell Albert not to persist.

Albert could show an unpleasantly priggish side of his character in the drawing-room after dinner. The Queen sometimes enjoyed gossipy small talk with her circle, but her husband would show his displeasure by withdrawing to a corner and playing double chess. Melbourne, whose biography by Lord David Cecil has enriched us all, commented on Albert with the cynicism of the Whig aristocrat who has seen all (including his wife, Caroline Lamb, making a fool of herself with Byron) – 'his damned morality will undo us all'.

But Albert's influence on the Queen became ever more pervasive. He did not like State functions, or guests and he would tell Victoria to refuse to invite even State visitors recommended by the government of the day. 'No Prince comes to this Palace,' wrote the Queen, 'unless he is a very near relation or particular friend.'

The image of Queen Victoria that the world recalls is of a short, dumpy woman enveloped in voluminous swathes of funereal black and wearing a matching expression of deep gloom. It is because, after the death of Albert in 1861, she donned widow's weeds for the next forty years.

In the early years of her reign she had been a different person – vivacious, social, always making sure there was plenty of company in the evening. The State rooms of Buckingham Palace saw more colour, laughter and gaiety for a few years than they probably were ever to experience again. The rooms created by George IV and Nash were used as rooms – not museum pieces. In the gold glitter of the Music Room Victoria took part in a 'regular old English dance' of seventy-two couples. They were usually still dancing at three in the morning. There were great balls with hundreds of guests and the dining-room was laid out as a supper-room and the Throne Room as a tea-room. After dancing all night one of the Queen's joys was to go out on the balcony of the Green Drawing-Room and watch the sun rise over St Paul's Cathedral.

Victoria was, after all, a child of the Regency with its roots in the lusty eighteenth century. All this side of her character, however, gradually disappeared after her marriage to Albert. 'The Victorian Age' dawned. It could more accurately, perhaps, be called 'The Age of Albert'.

Victoria was quite lucky that Buckingham Palace had survived to be a royal residence when she came to the throne. After the death of George IV in 1830 there were several moves to abandon the uncompleted Palace since costs had risen to a degree that angered both Parliament and public.

Nash was speedily dismissed and although nearly eighty years old was subjected to close, hostile questioning by a select committee. Between 1826 and 1830 Parliament had approved grants for the Palace of £496,000. It was now discovered that in fact £613,296-8-9d had been paid out. The total cost of completing the Palace was estimated at £644,473-8-9d.* Nash was not found guilty of personal dishonesty and was able to show he had for the most part merely

---

*It is not easy to compare the value of a pound sterling then and now, but a reasonably accurate estimate is that £650,000 in the 1830s would now be the equivalent of £1,625,000,000 (i.e. well over 1½ billion pounds).

Queen Victoria and Prince Albert in wig and powder. The period selected for this 'bal costume', held at Buckingham Palace in June 1845, was 1740–1750.

carried out the King's orders. There were, however, doubts about some of his deals with contractors and the enquiry cast a shadow over the last years of a man whose genius as a town-planner created areas of elegant grandeur in London that are now a treasured part of our national heritage.

William IV, who had succeeded his elder brother George, was a man of relatively simple tastes and had no wish to involve himself in the embarrassing problems of completing the Palace. He was quite

Queen Victoria and Prince Albert were both enthusiastic patrons of the arts. This engraving from *The Illustrated London News* shows a State concert in the Grand Saloon at Buckingham Palace on 28 May 1851. The Grand Saloon is on the western (garden) side of the Palace, and is between the State Ballroom and the White Drawing-Room. The Queen had a private orchestra which played both at Windsor and Buckingham Palace. The Grand Saloon has now become known as the Music Room.

49

happy living in Clarence House with the use of the adjoining St James's Palace for royal functions.

Among the alternative plans was a project to turn the Palace into a barracks which it was estimated would house three battalions of foot guards. Another idea was to 'privatise' the site, as might be said today, and sell it off as building plots. A more serious threat came in 1834 when the Houses of Parliament burned down and William IV eagerly offered the Palace as a replacement. He told the Speaker: 'I mean Buckingham House as a permanent gift. Mind that!'

The politicians and the influential men of the country had, however, sensed for a generation or more that there ought to be a new royal residence in London which would symbolise the growing power and wealth of the nation. The Marble Arch itself was to commemorate Trafalgar (1805) and Waterloo (1815), the key victories by sea and land which not only defeated Napoleon, but made possible the worldwide hegemony Britain was to enjoy in the nineteenth century.

Sir John Soane, a distinguished architect with official royal duties, produced a design for a magnificent 'Palace on Constitution Hill' which was exhibited at the Royal Academy as early as 1821. George IV toyed with the plans as late as 1827 at a time when Nash, his favourite architect, was already embarked on building a Palace around the Queen's House. It was, however, designed to be no more than a private residence with St James's still functioning for official duties. But, in spite of all the difficulties, Buckingham Palace was finally completed.

In this early period of Victoria's reign there were splendid social occasions every year at the Palace during 'the Season', even if Albert commented wistfully to Uncle Leopold, 'God be merciful to us miserable sinners!' There were at least two annual State balls attended by everyone who 'mattered' in society. These occasions really had glamour. The men were peacocks in their full-dress uniforms or court dress, adorned with decorations and orders. The women flowered in their magnificent gowns of rustling silk and glittered with diamonds, rubies and sapphires. Quite often there were over 1000 guests at the ball.

Victoria had a theatrical side to her character and was stimulated by such events, but especially by one of the great costume balls she gave. The first and most memorable was the fantastically costly and elaborate 'Plantagenet' ball on 12 May 1842, when Victoria and Albert assumed the roles of Edward III and Queen Philippa. Courtiers and guests were commanded to appear in appropriate fourteenth-century

At the Plantagenet costume ball held on 12 May 1842, Prince Albert appeared as Edward III and Queen Victoria as Queen Philippa.

costume and vied with each other in display. Albert became interested, studied the historical details meticulously and organised the preparations. Victoria finally declared that there were 'so many silks and drawings and crowns and God knows what to look at that I who hate being troubled about dress am quite "confuse"'.

The ball was one of the greatest spectacles the Palace was ever to witness: 'Such a scene,' remarked a spectator, 'may never occur again until Domesday.' A reasonable assumption, since the total expenditure (a joy to the tradesmen of London!), would now total tens of millions.

But the Palace began to play a lesser role once Albert had finished building Osborne by 1848. Victoria now expected her ministers to make the journey to the Isle of Wight by rail and ferry to attend to necessary matters of State.

Albert was soon to embark on his second building project – Balmoral Castle on Deeside in the Highlands which with its romantic forests and hills reminded him of his German homeland. Victoria and Albert first leased the property in 1848 and found increasing happiness there. They bought it in 1852 and began to rebuild the Castle which is still today a beloved home of the Royal Family. They say that if Queen Elizabeth II ever retired she would choose Balmoral as her home.

For Albert, the Castle and surrounding estate gave him another opportunity to draw the Queen and their growing family away from the outside world. In just a few years he had been remarkably successful in creating a private life for the British Royal Family. At Windsor it was comparatively easy to keep out of the limelight. The time spent at Buckingham Palace could now be restricted to the performance of inescapable duties and essential events.

It is worth recalling that Albert was inspired to build Osborne because the view reminded him of the Bay of Naples, and Balmoral because the landscape recalled Germany. He could not be said to have been enamoured of the beauties of the land of his adoption!

It was, however, in London at his desk in Buckingham Palace that Albert developed the most important project of his career – the Great Exhibition of 1851, which was presented with brilliant originality in Hyde Park within the immense glass structure of the Crystal Palace. Albert overcame the negative influences of inertia and stupid criticism to create an historic display which marked almost the apogee of British industrial and scientific genius. The outstanding success of the exhibition largely financed the great cultural and educational institutions which stretch down from the Albert Hall to

South Kensington. It is right that his elaborate memorial should stand in the Park overlooking these lasting achievements of his energy and imagination.

The balcony of the new east façade, which has now become so familiar, began to be used by Victoria soon after its completion. She took position there with some of the family on 18 November 1852, to watch the funeral cortège of the Duke of Wellington, which will be remembered for all time as one of the great pageants of her reign. Two years later, on 28 February 1854, she rose early and with her family went out on to the balcony to see the final battalion of the Guards march away to embark for the Crimea. 'It was,' she wrote, 'a touching and beautiful sight.'

Two years later, in May 1856, the new ballroom was used for the first time to celebrate what was called the victory of the Crimean campaign. In July the Queen was out on the balcony again to watch the returning troops march from Vauxhall to Hyde Park. Later in the day she rode out of the Palace mounted on a grey roan and wearing a scarlet jacket and black habit for a review of her troops and the presentation of the first newly-created Victoria Crosses.

Victoria gave birth at the Palace to her ninth and last child, Princess Beatrice, on 14 April 1857. In January of the next year her first child, Victoria ('Vicky'), the Princess Royal, was married to a future Kaiser of Germany. 'Vicky', intelligent, lively, adored by her father, was only seventeen and had been betrothed for nearly three years. The Palace was *en fête* for a week with balls and receptions and it was difficult to find rooms for all the royalty of Europe who had been invited. After the marriage in St James's Chapel, bride and bridegroom with the close relatives went out on the balcony to acknowledge the cheers of the crowds and so began an agreeable tradition recently renewed by the Prince of Wales and his Princess on 29 July 1981.

'Vicky's' marriage was the occasion of the last series of joyous events in the Palace for many years. As for 'Vicky', she faced a difficult life in Berlin, distrusted by the Germans as 'that English woman'. Her husband, a liberal-minded man, died tragically of

*Overleaf:* In 1851 the reign of Victoria came into full flower with the un-believably successful Great Exhibition. This picture shows the Queen leaving Buckingham Palace for the State opening on 1 May 1851.

cancer soon after he succeeded. Their son, Kaiser Wilhelm II, came with his Empress to the unveiling in 1911 of the massive Queen Victoria Memorial which stands on its island site in front of the Palace. The Kaiser was the eldest grandson of Queen Victoria and was devoted to her as he showed at her death.

In a curious, ambivalent way the man who was to lead Germany three years later into the 1914–18 war had an affection for this country. Before he left the Palace in 1911 he asked King George V if he could stand at the window of the room that gives on to the balcony where his mother and father had stood happily on their wedding day. When he returned his eyes were filled with tears. It was his last visit to England.

Albert died in the late evening of 14 December 1861, at Windsor. It was natural that the Queen should be distraught with grief at the loss of an adored husband. She was, however, only forty-two and was to live in good health for another forty years. She had children to care for, was monarch of a great country and a worldwide empire. Yet she wore her mourning permanently and withdrew from public life as much as possible.

In this pathological state of mind Buckingham Palace was, except for a few short, grudging appearances, excised from Victoria's life. The blinds were drawn, the carpets rolled up, the chandeliers and furniture covered. In the airless rooms there developed a close

*Previous page:* On 13 June 1851, a few weeks after the opening of the Great Exhibition, another State ball was held at Buckingham Palace. It was designed to give an impetus to the trade of the metropolis, and took the form of a costume ball, this time in the period of Charles II.

*Above:* Prince Albert died on 14 December 1861 at Windsor. This engraving shows him with Queen Victoria at the last 'Drawing-Room' held before his death.

*Below:* The Throne Room is now rarely used. But in Queen Victoria's reign Loyal Addresses were presented here in great splendour by certain privileged bodies such as the Universities of Oxford and Cambridge. In this engraving from *The Illustrated London News*, the Archbishop of Canterbury, Primate of the Church of England – of which the sovereign is the Supreme Governor – presents an Address of the Convocation of the Clergy on 16 February 1853.

atmosphere of stale mustiness which they say still pervades certain rooms even to this day.

Victoria, with an almost total disregard for public opinion, organised her life so that she spent four months of the year at Osborne, four months at Windsor and four months at Balmoral. Prince Albert's rooms were by the Queen's strict commands preserved exactly as he had left them with essential dusting and cleaning done under close supervision. Throughout the Palace nothing was changed. If anything broke or wore out it had to be replaced identically. As time passed the endless corridors and suites of rooms sank into a lifeless mausoleum and dampened the spirits of

*Previous page:* This engraving from *The Illustrated London News* shows the first Drawing-Room of the season, on 24 March 1860, at Buckingham Palace. Four Drawing-Rooms were usually held every year, two before and two after Easter. This was when débutantes were presented at court, usually by mother, relative or friend.

This 'Drawing-Room' at Buckingham Palace was held in March 1874. 'Drawing-Rooms' provided a system of access to the sovereign and other members of her House. In publishing this engraving, *The Graphic* informed readers that a few years previously – when 'Drawing-Rooms' were held at the old Palace of St James – 'owing to the large number of persons who were deemed worthy of presentation to the Queen, which was due to the increase of wealth and population, the scene was wont to resemble that at the gallery door of a theatre on Boxing Night. After all the care ladies bestowed on their attire their clothes were nearly torn off their backs in their struggles to reach the royal presence, and the floors were strewn with ostrich feathers, fragments of costly lace, and ornaments of jewellery!'

the royal relatives whom the Queen allowed to use the Palace, more or less as an hotel, when they visited London.

The State balls and concerts continued to be held during the short London season with the Prince of Wales acting for his mother. From 1864 she held her courts at Buckingham Palace, but these formal daytime receptions were dull affairs with no music, food or drink. From 1866 she put in an appearance for half-an-hour or so at the Drawing-Rooms when the débutantes were presented. She came up from Windsor for these occasions, but returned the same day.

She was at the christening in the Palace chapel of the first-born of the Prince and Princess of Wales, the ill-fated Duke of Clarence, on 10 March 1864. She still did not stay, however, even for the cold collation that followed. In 1872 she did appear with the Prince of Wales on the Palace balcony after the Thanksgiving Service at St Paul's on 27 February, which marked his recovery from a dangerous bout of typhoid.

In the summer of 1887 the Palace came briefly to life again for the celebrations of the Queen's Golden Jubilee. On 21 June, Victoria rode out of the Palace in her state carriage drawn by eight cream-coloured ponies to a service in Westminster Abbey. After that year the Queen, who had been moved by the enthusiasm of the crowds, came up to the Palace now and again for a royal wedding and in July 1893, came out on the balcony with the Duke and Duchess of York (the future King George V and Queen Mary) after their marriage in the Chapel Royal of St James's.

The climax, however, came in June 1897. She slept in the Palace on the night of the nineteenth and woke up the next morning to celebrate sixty years on the throne – a reign longer than any other monarch of the country. The Diamond Jubilee was celebrated

If building the east façade did nothing else, it provided the world-famous balcony from which the population could see the Royal Family and vice versa. Here is an early engraving from *The Graphic* published in March 1874. (*Above*)

The Queen's Garden-Party at Buckingham Palace in July 1896.

*Overleaf:* The Queen leaving Buckingham Palace in her carriage in 1897, the year of her Diamond Jubilee.

publicly two days later when she set out behind contingents of troops from her worldwide Empire and was followed by the sixteen royal carriages needed for her descendants on her triumphant drive through London to St Paul's.

She was in an open landau, drawn again by the famous cream-coloured ponies and for this supreme day she put aside her widow's weeds and wore a grey silk gown, embroidered in silver, and a bonnet in which white flowers lightened the black lace. It was a sunny day and she held a parasol over her head as she drove through crowds greater than anyone believed possible. She did not leave the carriage but by the steps of the Cathedral, with Alexandra, the Princess of Wales, by her side, she listened to the voices of 500 choristers and the prayers of thanksgiving intoned by the clergy, led by the Archbishop of Canterbury. Later in the day she was glimpsed momentarily at the window of the balcony. In the evening she

*Previous page:* Queen Victoria's last appearance on the balcony was in March 1900 following the relief of Ladysmith during the Boer War. Thousands of people assembled at the Palace and serenaded the Queen by singing patriotic songs.

*Above:* In June 1897 Queen Victoria celebrated her Diamond Jubilee. For this supreme day she put aside her widow's weeds and wore a grey silk gown, embroidered in silver, and a bonnet in which white flowers lightened the black lace.

*Right:* On 22 January 1901 Queen Victoria died at Osborne, surrounded by many of her family. Even more of her 'wider family' gathered outside Buckingham Palace to read the notices displayed there.

presided at the family banquet in the State Dining-Room. The table had been extended as far as it would go and was decorated with a tower of 50,000 orchids grown in countries of the Empire.

The next day, before she left for Windsor, she was able – by a technological marvel of the day – to press a button in the Palace which flashed a message round the world: 'From my heart I thank my beloved people. May God bless them.'

She made her last appearance on the balcony in March 1900, when she acknowledged the vast crowds celebrating the relief of Ladysmith in South Africa with the hysteria that marked popular response to the unjust war against the Boer Republics. In May of the same year she held her last Drawing-Room. On 22 January 1901, she died at Osborne surrounded by many of her family, including the Prince of Wales, who succeeded as Edward VII.


## EDWARD VII

The new King took his time about moving into Buckingham Palace. It was not until 12 April 1902, fifteen months after his accession, that he and Queen Alexandra took up residence there.

One of the reasons was that the King wanted the Palace to be cleared of the piles of accumulated debris and then thoroughly cleaned and decorated. Albert's rooms were dismantled and Edward in time gave away some of the contents as mementoes to members of the family. There had been only some electric light in the Palace, now it was installed throughout. More bathrooms and lavatories were built and in the principal suites three wash-basins were lavished in a row – one for washing teeth, one for the hands and one for the face. Edward, who was in his sixties, was not a great innovator, but he had these changes made for comfort and luxury. The numerous household staff which had for many years been ridiculously under-employed was now more or less earning its keep again with the Royal Family now in residence and giving State functions and hospitality.

The King did, however, dispense with the services of a richly-uniformed upper servant whom he noticed stood by the sideboard every evening at dinner without performing any duties. He made enquiries and was told he was the official wine-taster, but was not now called upon to perform his task as the danger of poison being introduced into the royal cup was no longer considered likely. His salary was £600 p.a. which, with board and keep, would by today's values be envied by many. The King, in his generous-hearted way, ensured that he was found other duties. This open-handed, outward-looking attitude towards life did much in time to enhance the popularity of the monarchy. Victoria in her later years, although revered, acquired the reputation of being close with money and this did not endear her to the tradesmen and lower orders.

The débutantes who were presented each year at Court to gain the coveted seal of social eligibility were given much greater opportunity to show their wares by a monarch who was known to like women. Instead of the old stiff afternoon 'Drawing-Rooms', there were evening receptions where courtiers escorted the young women to the thrones in the ballroom where the King and Queen graciously acknowledged their curtsies. It was all much more exciting and gave the debs the opportunity of wearing more elaborate gowns and rich trains, more lavish jewellery and larger sprays of ostrich feathers. It was all part of the Edwardian ostentation and slightly vulgar show-off. After the presentation the girls moved into adjoining State rooms where food and drink restored them and their relatives after the nervous tensions of weeks (perhaps years!) of expensive preparation.

King Edward opened up the Palace to the men and women who had long been part of his 'Marlborough set' of which his mother had so strongly disapproved. The surviving 'Old Guard' of Victoria's court, both male and female, might sniff haughtily and shrug their shoulders despairingly, but the King's friends, many of them Jews of the new, City stock exchange plutocracy, brought a new liveliness and shrewd European intelligence to the Palace. Newspaper proprietors, editors, financiers, industrialists rubbed shoulders with members of the old aristocracy who were the King's cronies – men who gambled, kept a string or two of horses and women, and in the shooting season invited the King to their vast country houses where he spent the day eating, drinking and aiming at clouds of driven birds, and the night with his current mistress. It was slightly raffish, at times 'caddish', but then this was the Edwardian age and, like the women's fashions, rather extravagant.

It was the world of the Rothschilds of the third generation and of such men as Sir Ernest Cassel, the financier, who came from Germany to make a vast fortune in England and became probably the most intimate friend and astute adviser of the King. Cassel's grand-daughter, Edwina, in time inherited his great fortune and married Lord Louis (the future Earl) Mountbatten. So, as it turned out, Cassel was linked posthumously to the Royal Family when

8500 BUCKINGHAM PALACE

Prince Philip Mountbatten married Princess Elizabeth, who was soon to succeed to the throne as Queen Elizabeth II.

The great balls, banquets and receptions brought life back to the Palace after the decades of emptiness. The superb gowns and jewellery of the women, the uniforms, court dress, sashes and decorations once more enlivened the State Apartments. But although this was a new century, the twentieth, there was in the air a mood more of decadent *fin de siècle*, and an atmosphere of jaded age desperately clinging to pleasure rather than youth freely tasting life's joys.

The King did his best to restore a royal presence, majestic, yet popular, to the Palace which had been neglected for so long by his mother. He largely succeeded. Since his reign, Buckingham Palace has reigned physically and symbolically as the centre of the British monarchy. Yet, ironically, he was never at ease there and at times seized by moods of dark depression he could not shake off. There was music, beautiful women, stimulating talk, every exquisite choice of food and wine, but there was also haunting unhappiness for the King.

There were memories of unhappy childhood years when he had found it a torture to try and attain the high standards expected by his father. There were memories of humiliation when he had met ministers at Palace balls and concerts during the endless widowhood knowing that they had been forbidden by the Queen to engage him in anything more than small talk. There were memories of the unhealthy worship of his father's memory that he had tried to banish from the Palace, but which at times affected him even physically. Bitterly he would refer to the Palace as 'the sepulchre' and there were nights after the music had stopped and his guests had departed when they say he saw his mother's ghost, heard her voice and the tap of her stick.

Despairing of living happily in the Palace the King enquired whether it would be possible to move the court, lock, stock and barrel, to Hampton Court Palace, which had almost no associations with Victoria nor Albert. After studies had been made the plan was abandoned because of the great cost and the administrative

*Previous page:* The Mall or east front of the Palace in 1905. Eight years later, because the stone had deteriorated in the polluted atmosphere of Victorian and Edwardian London, the whole façade was re-faced after the design of Sir Aston Webb.

difficulties which would be caused by the distance from the centre of London.

The best he could do was to organise his life so that he spent as little time as possible at the Palace, without neglecting his essential duties. He would spend Christmas and the New Year at Sandringham, his own home in Norfolk. During January there were shooting parties both there and on friends' estates. At the end of the month he would come to London to open Parliament and in February, apart from entertaining at the Palace, his time would be spent going out to dinners, the theatre and supper parties. At the beginning of March he would spend a week in Paris and then on to Biarritz for three weeks to be joined by Mrs Keppel. He then cruised for a month in the royal yacht, generally in the Mediterranean.

He would return to Buckingham Palace towards the end of May and preside over the few crowded weeks of 'the Season'. In June it was off to Windsor for the Ascot races and at the beginning of July a visit for two or three days to some provincial centre. Then it was time for Goodwood and Cowes, followed by a month at Marienbad in Bohemia for the cure which also included some discreet pleasures. He would then return to the Palace for a few days, before going to stay with his friends, the Saviles, for the Doncaster races. In October he would be at Balmoral, with a break for the autumn meeting at Newmarket. In December, he was back at Sandringham for a week and then to Buckingham Palace for two weeks of theatres and parties before returning to Norfolk for Christmas.

This programme ensured that at the most he would spend no more than about three months of the year at the Palace. Fate, however, caught up with him, for he died in the Palace he so disliked on 6 May 1910.

## GEORGE V

King George was forty-five when he came to the Throne, and Queen Mary forty-three. They had five sons* and a daughter. The King – whose long, hard years as a boy in the Navy had moulded him – was dutiful, dull and hated change. Mary (May, as she was known) was the daughter of Princess Mary Adelaide, a cousin of Queen Victoria,

*This includes Prince John who was born in 1905 with such handicaps that his death in 1919 was considered merciful.

whose reckless extravagance aided by that of her charming, penniless husband, Prince Franz of Teck, sent them into exile to Florence for a few years. Princess May, who was in her teens, flowered there and acquired not only a knowledge of the arts, but also an understanding of a world wider than that of the apartments of Kensington Palace in which she had been born and brought up.

Her marriage to George followed an earlier engagement to his elder brother, Prince Eddy. On his early death Victoria determined that May, whose good looks and strong physique promised well for the Royal Family, should marry the next-in-line. So, in time, Mary did become Queen, enabling her to play a role of splendour at the high price of many years' frustrating submissiveness.

The King and Queen settled down in their suites of rooms on the first floor of the north wing facing Green Park. They have by custom become the living quarters of the Royal Family today. After living in Marlborough House, the 'most perfect of all houses', the Queen found the Palace 'straggly, such distances to go and so fatiguing'. It took her time to come to terms with the endless red-carpeted corridors and the claustrophobic atmosphere.

She not only came to terms with the Palace, however, she became the one person since it was built to understand what George IV and Nash had been about. Because she was Queen and mistress of the Palace, she was able over the years to ensure that its concept was not only preserved in a vulgar, iconoclastic century, but also enhanced by her understanding, study and taste, together with judicious purchases. She is, therefore, a central figure in the history of Buckingham Palace.

One of her most memorable improvements was the transformation of the dark, gloomy, overcrowded Picture Gallery into the splendid, well-lit background for carefully-hung paintings that it is today.

Queen Mary was never allowed to have any influence, however, on the King's study. It was dark, almost dingy, and cluttered up with innumerable objects from framed photographs, mementoes, reference books, gifts, old diaries, and useless bits of china. Woebetide the servant who in dusting replaced one item out of place! The King knew exactly where everything ought to be. Alongside the plain roll-top desk where he worked was a large birdcage for his parrot, Charlotte. She was a constant companion and he would often let her out to fly around and even peck at food in the private dining-room. It was as if he was playing the part of the old tar with a parrot on his shoulder. At the far end of the room was a fireplace behind a large screen and here the King would often sit after dinner, sometimes alone, sometimes with one of his old cronies at the other side of the hearth.

The study, however, was not all quiet work and genial conversation. Here the King would summon his sons who had incurred his wrath. It was more often than not the eldest, David (to the family), the Prince of Wales, later King Edward VIII, and on his abdication, Duke of Windsor.

The King was gruff and unsympathetic to all his sons, but David's easy, unconventional manner, his insouciant charm which made him in time the nation's idol, and his refusal to marry an eligible princess or aristocrat – in fact the entire attitude to life of his eldest son enraged him. He would upbraid him in the coarse language he had learned as a boy in the Navy, almost shaking with fury as he shouted his abuse. It is not surprising that the Prince came to hate the Palace.

In George V's reign of twenty-six years (1910–36) the Palace was the scene of two momentous events which marked the passing of an old world that had seemed secure and the emergence of a new one that was sailing into uncharted, dangerous seas.

On the evening of Tuesday, 4 August 1914, it was known that the British ultimatum to Germany would expire at 11 p.m. (midnight in Berlin). Great crowds had been gathering during the evening in the centre of London and moved, as if by instinct, towards Buckingham Palace, although its windows showed no light. Over at Westminster, Big Ben struck the fatal hour. The crowds outside the Palace stood blindly waiting – for what could they expect? Then the curtains of the room behind the balcony were drawn back and the lights shone like a beacon into the night. A footman in magnificent livery opened the windows. The King and Queen stepped out on to the balcony as if on to a stage. The appearance was not designed to raise war-like emotions, rather to calm anxiety. It did not last long and slowly the crowds faded away into the night.

The darkness that fell over the world was to destroy the old structure of Europe for ever. When George V stepped out on to the balcony, there were three other monarchs of his rank and importance – his cousin, Nicholas II, the Tsar of Russia, our ally in this war, another cousin, Wilhelm II, Emperor of Germany, our principal enemy, and another enemy, Franz Josef, Emperor of Austria, Hungary and many other lands.

Four years and three months later, on 11 November 1918, George and Mary stepped out on to the same Palace balcony to rejoice with the massive crowds cheering the news of the Armistice which marked the victorious end to the war.

*Opposite, above:* Buckingham House as it looked for most of the reign of George III until the rebuilding by his son George IV who employed the great architect John Nash. Throughout this period the House was a royal home. The court was at St James's Palace where it remained until Queen Victoria's Reign.

The simple elegance of Buckingham House is seen in this fine water-colour by W. Westall. In his quest for privacy, George III erected iron railings along the entire front of the House.

*Opposite, below:* This winter scene of Buckingham Palace, a colour litho-graph published by R. Havell and Son from a drawing by J. Burnett, shows the Palace prior to the building of the east façade. Queen Victoria arrived at the Palace for the first time in July 1837 and drove through the gleaming Marble Arch which was removed when the east façade was built in 1847–50.

*Overleaf:* After the purchase of Balmoral Castle in 1852, the Royal Family spent less time at Buckingham Palace. But there were still inescapable ceremonial occasions to attend. Such was the banquet in the Picture Gallery on the occasion of the christening of Prince Leopold on 28 June 1853, depicted in this watercolour by Louis Haghe.

*Opposite:* There were splendid social occasions at Buckingham Palace during The Season in the early period of Queen Victoria's reign. This watercolour by Eugene Louis Lami shows the crowded Grand Staircase at the State Ball of 5 July 1848.

*Overleaf:* Queen Mary did much to restore the Palace to the original conception of King George IV and his architect John Nash. One of her most memorable improvements was the transformation of the formerly dark and overcrowded Picture Gallery.

Eight million young men had lost their lives in that war. With the deaths from epidemics, famine and revolutions probably twenty-five million had died as a consequence of the conflict.

Of the four monarchs who had ruled Empires in 1914, George V was now the only one who was still with a throne. The Kaiser had abdicated and gone into exile. The Hohenzollerns had no more part to play in Germany. The same fate had come to the successor of Franz Josef. The Habsburgs were no more in Vienna. As for the House of Romanoff, the Tsar and his immediate family had been murdered in July 1918 at Ekaterinburg where they had been held prisoners following the Russian Revolution of 1917.

All over Europe minor monarchies were falling. Revolution was in the air. King George, who in 1917 had changed the German family name to the quintessentially English Windsor, faced the future with anxiety and wondered how stable even Britain and the monarchy might be in the coming years. He need not have worried. In spite of bitter industrial disputes, including a General Strike in 1926, in spite of a prolonged economic depression in the thirties with millions of unemployed and their families suffering privation, Britain remained a remarkably stable society with the monarchy as revered and popular as ever.

The gruff, old King quietly working away for eight months of the year at his desk in Buckingham Palace had won respect and growing affection. When he and Queen Mary celebrated the Silver Jubilee of their reign on 6 May 1935 the enthusiastic warmth of the crowds quite amazed him: 'I'd no idea they felt like that about me,' he said, 'I am beginning to think they must really like me for myself.'

The Jubilee gave the Palace an opportunity to take part in a vital development in communications. Queen Victoria had sent her Diamond Jubilee message round the world from the Palace by electric telegraph. Now her grandson, George, sat in front of a microphone

*Previous page:* When King George V and Queen Mary celebrated the Silver Jubilee of their reign on 6 May 1935, the enthusiastic warmth of the crowds quite amazed him. In his radio broadcast to the nation from the Palace he repeated Queen Victoria's words at her Diamond Jubilee: 'From my heart I thank my beloved people. May God bless them.'

in the same Palace and broadcast his Silver Jubilee message by radio and the world was able to listen to his voice. It was, however, in keeping with his sense of tradition that he ended the message with the same words Victoria had used: 'From my heart I thank my beloved people. May God bless them.'

# EDWARD VIII

King George V died at Sandringham on 20 January 1936 and was succeeded by his heir to the throne who took the title of Edward VIII. On 10 December of the same year he abdicated to be able to marry Mrs Wallis Simpson, the twice divorced American woman with whom he had fallen in love.

When he was in London the new King at first continued to live at York House, adjoining St James's Palace. He had an office, however, in Buckingham Palace, choosing a somewhat obscure room on the ground floor of the north wing. It faced inwards to the quadrangle and had poor light, but it was near the offices of his principal officials and he soon established an informal but efficient way of getting through the business of the day. He proved himself the most accessible of kings.

His mother, Queen Mary, remained in Buckingham Palace until the autumn whilst Marlborough House was being made ready for her again. When she left, Edward moved into the Palace and once more broke with the recent past, choosing to occupy the splendid ground-floor suite of rooms at the north end of the garden front. They had been designed by Nash as the private apartments of George IV and are worthy of a monarch. In Queen Victoria's time they acquired the name of 'the Belgian Suite' for they were often occupied by King Leopold of Belgium, uncle to both the Queen and Prince Albert, whose marriage he had planned with some cunning. The name of the suite has stuck and over the years it has accommodated the very grandest visitors to the Palace.

Before he moved in, King Edward had the bathroom modernised and a shower installed. He also replaced the massive ornate State bedstead with a more modest bed. It was, however, already October when he took up residence. Within a few weeks the marriage crisis broke and he was gone, leaving almost no more trace than a hotel guest.

## GEORGE VI

The new King, who thus unexpectedly came to the throne, was a few days short of his forty-first birthday. He had never been strong, and suffered from a bad stammer which he overcame by dogged perseverance. Naturally shy, George, as the second son, had lived peacefully enough as Duke of York in the shadow of his glamorous elder brother. His greatest piece of luck had been to persuade Elizabeth Bowes-Lyon, five years younger than he and daughter of the 14th Earl of Strathmore, to marry him – 'You'll be a lucky fellow if she accepts you,' his father told him. Her charm and warmth of personality were fortunately matched by the strength of her character. Without her it is difficult to imagine how Prince Albert (as he was named) could have coped as King during the taxing years of his reign dominated as they were by the perilous war of 1939–45.

George and Elizabeth moved into the Palace in February 1937 and occupied the same apartments as his father and mother. Their two daughters, Elizabeth (now Queen Elizabeth II) and Margaret, followed in a few weeks. Elizabeth was nearly eleven years old and Margaret, six and a half.

There is an excellent account of a dinner-party given for about twenty the following month at the Palace by one of the guests, Harold Nicolson.* Although Nicolson was a member of the establishment (a former diplomat and son of a distinguished diplomat), and married into an aristocratic family, he was obviously somewhat overwhelmed by the magnificence of the occasion when he arrived in his knee-breeches and silk stockings punctually at 8.20 p.m. on 17 March 1937. He passed through an outer and inner hall and . . . 'I then go upstairs a little alarmed by the fact that upon each fourth step stands a footman dressed in scarlet and gold epaulettes and powdered about the hair.'

In the first Drawing-Room the equerries and ladies-in-waiting are in attendance as the guests arrive and a very distinguished gathering it is – Baldwin, the Prime Minister, Lloyd George, a former Prime Minister, Lord Halifax, a former Viceroy and future Foreign Secretary, Montagu Norman, Governor of the Bank of England, the Duke of Rutland, the Duke of Buccleuch, Lord David Cecil and a

---

*Harold Nicolson, *Diaries and Letters*, 1930–1939. Collins, 1966.

Looking up The Mall to the east front of Buckingham Palace. This is the view of the Palace best known to the world at large since the unveiling by King George V in 1911 of the statue in honour of Queen Victoria.

cabinet minister or two. Their wives are in full fig, some with tiaras glittering in their coiffures.

The guests are then ushered into another Drawing-Room and arranged in the appropriate order. At 8.45 the King and Queen enter silently and shake hands all round. The equerries then approach the Duchess of Rutland and Mr Baldwin and lead them to the King and Queen who are now waiting to lead the procession to the State Dining-Room. The King escorts the Duchess. The Queen extends her arm to the Prime Minister.

As the party approaches the Dining-Room the band of the Grenadier Guards in the room beyond strikes up 'God Save the King' and Nicolson and others, not in the know, wonder whether they should halt and stand to attention.

'The dining-table,' Nicolson continues, 'is one mass of gold candelabra and scarlet tulips. Behind us the whole of the Windsor (gold) plate is massed in tiers. The dinner has been unwisely selected since we have soup, fish, quail, ham, chicken, ice and savoury. The wine, on the other hand, is excellent and the port superb. When we have finished our savoury the King rises and we all resume our procession back to the drawing-rooms.'

At the fourth Drawing-Room the equerries whisper to the men to leave their ladies and follow the King to another Drawing-Room for coffee and cigars. Then they join the Queen and the ladies in the Picture Gallery. The Queen goes the rounds and Nicolson praises her charm and dignity, even though she teased him on his pink face and pink views (he was then an M.P. of some consequence to the left of the Conservatives).

'Thereafter,' he ends, 'the Queen drops us a deep curtsey which is answered by all the ladies present. We then go away. . .'

Such hospitable grandeur displayed by the court at Buckingham Palace during that Coronation Year of 1937 proved, however, to be elegiac. The following year saw the threat of imminent war and in 1939 it broke out.

During the coronation celebrations, however, there was an atmosphere of almost daily excitement in the Palace as if it were making up for lost time and storing up happy memories for tragic years ahead. There were great State balls with over 2000 guests conducted with all the ritual of the Lord Chamberlain and other Household officers, carrying their wands of office, walking backwards as the King and Queen entered the State ballroom to the strains of the National Anthem. The dancing was opened by the royal couple and went on until the early hours while liveried footmen plied the guests with food and wine.

With presentation parties for débutantes, receptions and dinners, this coronation season would have delighted George IV, Nash – and the young Queen Victoria. For the new King and Queen such a brilliant first year gave false promise of a prosperous and happy future. It was not to be. For many of the young men in brilliant full-dress uniforms who danced the night away in the Palace ballroom that season there was not much time left – not much time at all.

When war broke out on 3 September 1939 the Palace was fairly well-prepared for the expected air attacks with basement shelters, stirrup pumps and buckets of sand. The art treasures of the Palace had been moved to safety and the pattern of life became utilitarian and, later, austere.

The two young Princesses spent the war in safety at Windsor. The King and Queen spent most weekends there and during the worst of

King George VI was operated on for lung cancer in September 1951. He is seen here with Queen Elizabeth leaving Buckingham Palace for the first time following his operation. After spending Christmas at Sandringham, he returned to the Palace once more before leaving for Sandringham where he died in his sleep in the early hours of 6 February 1952.

the bombing in 1940 and 1941 went down for a relatively quiet night's sleep. But both spent much time in London, carrying out their duties in the Palace, visiting the worst bombed areas and giving what comfort and sympathy they could to the wounded, the bereaved and those who had lost their homes. Such visits in London and in the provinces forged new links of loyalty with the King and Queen – 'they were there!'

In September 1940, when London suffered so badly, the Palace was hit several times and the chapel was severely damaged. In the following March bombs fell in the forecourt and on North Lodge. One of the policemen died on his way to hospital. In 1944 a V1 hit a tree in the Palace gardens, wrecked a summer-house and blew out some windows, but no one was injured.

So on VE Day, 8 May 1945, the Palace may have borne its scars and some windows may have been boarded up, but it was still there! Britain was, however, impoverished and exhausted and there was only a gradual – very gradual – return to a peacetime routine at the Palace – one that would never match the old way of life.

The King's health began to fail seriously at the end of 1947 following a long, exhausting tour of South Africa with the Queen and the two Princesses. He carried on with tenacity until the autumn of 1951 when the doctors diagnosed lung cancer. The operation to remove the left lung took place on 23 September and was successful, but it left him very weak. On 21 December he celebrated his fifty-sixth birthday with his family in Buckingham Palace. After Christmas at Sandringham he returned to London and went with the whole family to see *South Pacific* at Drury Lane. The next day he drove to London Airport to wave goodbye to Elizabeth and Philip who were setting off on a long tour which was to take them to East Africa, Australia and New Zealand.

In the press photographs the King looked tired and strained. He then left for Sandringham again and the Palace was to see him no

The Queen Mother at Clarence House on the occasion of her eightieth birthday, 4 August 1980.
In 1949, the Queen (then Princess Elizabeth) and Philip moved into Clarence House and Princess Anne was born there the following year.
After the death of King George VI, the Queen Mother moved to Clarence House and has lived there ever since.

more. After a day's rough shooting on 5 February in cold, crisp weather, he dined, went to bed and died in his sleep early next day. It was a good end for a man who had, like his father, preferred the role of Squire of Sandringham to any other.


## QUEEN ELIZABETH II

The new Queen, who was twenty-five, moved into Buckingham Palace during 1952 with her husband, Prince Philip, and their two children, Charles and Anne. She has lived there longer than any other monarch. Victoria took up residence in the then new Palace in 1837, a few weeks after she came to the throne, but she virtually abandoned it in 1861 after the death of Prince Albert. She went on to reign until 1901, but she can be said to have lived in the Palace for no more than twenty-four years.

As for her successors, Edward VII was there for nine, George V for twenty-six, Edward VIII for less than a year and George VI for sixteen.

Elizabeth's links with the Palace go back much further, however, than the years she has lived there as Queen. She was christened there on 29 May 1926 in the private chapel which was later destroyed by German bombs. During her early years when her parents, then the Duke and Duchess of York, lived in a mansion in Piccadilly within sight of the Palace, Princess Elizabeth was a favoured visitor to her grandparents, King George V and Queen Mary, who remained especially close to her.

In early 1937 when she was nearly eleven, Elizabeth and her younger sister Margaret followed their parents, now King and Queen, to Buckingham Palace. They had nursery suites on the second floor of the north wing where their lives were organised by Alla, the senior nurse, Bobo, the nurserymaid to Elizabeth, and Crawfie, the governess.*

---

*'Alla' was Clara Knight who died in 1943.

'Bobo' was Margaret Macdonald, nurserymaid to Elizabeth since her birth in 1926, dresser since 1952, and who has become the closest confidante the Queen has ever made.

'Crawfie' was Miss Marion Crawford, governess to Elizabeth and Margaret from 1932–49. In 1950 she published a book, *The Little Princesses*, which had an enormous success and made a great deal of money. Although officially criticised for disclosing information obtained in a confidential position, the book did nothing but good for the Royal Family. Miss Crawford later married and went to live in Scotland not far from Balmoral.

When the King had a look at the old schoolroom above the balcony room on the second floor of the east front, he decided it was too dreary for his beloved daughters (whom he spoiled, especially Margaret) and had a brighter room decorated on the corner of the north wing, nearer their own rooms.

That first year of the new reign, 1937, was all excitement centred on the coronation in which Elizabeth and Margaret took a part. The Palace was filled with guests and Elizabeth, though so young, was already a person of importance for it was by then considered very likely that she would inherit the Crown.

When she returned to the Palace from the wartime years at Windsor she was a young woman, already deeply in love with Prince Philip. It was from the Palace that she was married on 20 November 1947 and returned with him from Westminster Abbey in a glass coach to a magnificent wedding breakfast graced by most of the reigning kings and queens and even more of those now in exile.

After the honeymoon Elizabeth and Philip returned to the Palace. They lived there with her parents for more than a year whilst Clarence House was being made ready for them after bomb damage and years of neglect. For a time they lived in the Belgian Suite, but both Elizabeth and Philip found its splendour overwhelming. They were both young and neither had any taste for living in rooms that were museum-pieces. Philip, especially, has taken a long time to come to terms with the Palace which he initially found gloomy and unfriendly. He had spent his life as an exile and had had little experience of palaces. The years of his youth, except for occasional visits to his grand relatives, the Mountbattens, had been spent in the more austere surroundings of his school at Gordonstoun in Scotland, the Royal Naval College at Dartmouth and aboard ships on active service during the War.

Elizabeth became pregnant and she and Philip moved into her old post-war suite on the second floor of the north-east corner. One of the old nurseries nearby was turned into a delivery room and there Prince Charles was born on 14 November 1948. As the chapel was unusable he was christened in the Music Room, but the traditional gold lily font was brought up from Windsor and Jordan water was sprinkled by the Archbishop of Canterbury.

*Overleaf:* At the start of her honeymoon in November 1947, Princess Elizabeth rides with her husband in the open landau taking her to Waterloo station.

In 1949 Elizabeth and Philip moved to Clarence House and Princess Anne was born there on 15 August 1950, but was taken across to the Palace to be christened, like Charles, in the Music Room.

Anne is the only one of the Queen's four children not to be born in the Palace. Andrew (19 February 1960) and Edward (10 March 1964), both saw the light of day in the bathroom of the Belgian Suite which, with its great ornate bath designed for George IV, had been made into a delivery room.

Childhood, youth, marriage, the birth of her three sons – all these have been part of the Queen's life in Buckingham Palace. But they are only a part. Here she has exercised her constitutional duties, among them giving audience to her Prime Ministers on Tuesday evenings when Parliament is in session. The list of names range from Churchill, Eden, Macmillan and Douglas-Home to Wilson, Heath, Callaghan and now, Margaret Thatcher. Here, at State banquets, she has entertained not only constitutional kings and queens, but rulers as varied as de Gaulle of France and Kosygin of Soviet Russia. Here she has held meetings with the leaders of the Commonwealth, which she has done so much to promote, both in Great Britain and on visits – and which may well prove to be her greatest achievement.

She has given lunch to the first man who circled the earth from space – the Russian, Major Gagarin – a man of modest, heroic quality. She has given hospitality to Billy Graham, the American evangelist who had gifts that seemed almost God-given when he came to Britain on the first of a series of, initially, enormously successful campaigns. In May 1982 as Queen and Supreme Governor of the Church of England, she greeted in her Palace Pope John Paul II when he made his historic visit to Britain. Indeed, the most significant events of the Queen's life have happened in the Palace against a background of investitures for the brave and the dutiful, garden-parties for thousands of guests, grand receptions for the diplomatic corps of the world, luncheon parties for those who are considered by her advisers to be significant in the life of the nation.

The Queen has worked hard and successfully in her Palace, surrounded by a staff of around 300 full-time and 120 part-time employees and protected by personal detectives, Special Branch and other policemen, as well as the Household Troops. Whatever dangers the Queen might face in the outside world, inside Buckingham Palace, and especially in her private apartments, she should feel safe.

Four generations of our Royal Family are shown in this photo by Baron taken in 1950: *from l. to r.* Queen Mary, the baby Princess Anne, Princess Elizabeth and Queen Elizabeth.

Princess Anne, born on 15 August 1950, was christened later that year in the Music Room of Buckingham Palace.

On 28 May 1982 The Queen welcomed Pope John Paul II at the Palace during his historic visit to Britain.

104

That sense of security was destroyed – perhaps for ever – on the morning of Friday, 9 July 1982 when she woke in the night to find an intruder wandering around her bedroom. Michael Fagan had not only evaded all the elaborate precautions designed to keep intruders out, but when he engaged the Queen in conversation as he sat on her bed, her attempts to summon help went unheeded.

Before studying these and other security and household matters, it is appropriate to describe the Palace as it is today with the aid of a reasonably accurate chart (*see overleaf*).

Buckingham Palace has rather more than 600 rooms. It is unwise to give a more definite figure for various surveys have over the years produced differing results depending on whether lobbies, pantries or even lavatories have been considered as 'rooms'.* The four wings of the Palace are built round a rather gloomy, gravelled quadrangle that the public has not been able to view since the east front, facing the Mall, was built in the time of Victoria and Albert. There is a basement and four floors – ground, principal, bedroom and attic. It is on the first (principal) floor of the north wing that the Queen and Prince Philip live when they are in residence.

The Queen spends around thirty weeks of the year in Buckingham Palace, but this figure is obviously flexible, depending on the length of foreign, Commonwealth and domestic tours. She invariably spends Christmas at Windsor followed by a stay at Sandringham until the beginning of February – a total, say, of six weeks. She has an Easter break of around four weeks at Windsor. In June she is back there for another week to attend the Royal Ascot meeting nearby. In July she is generally at the Goodwood meeting in Sussex staying with the Duke of Richmond and Gordon, who owns the course, or perhaps with the Duke of Norfolk at Arundel Castle, which is not far away. At the beginning of August she starts the ten-week-long family holiday at Balmoral, sometimes sailing up in the royal yacht, *Britannia* and visiting en route a significant development such as the North Sea oil-fields.

Since early in her reign (1954) the Queen has so organised her life that she spends only weekdays in Buckingham Palace, unless there is a crisis. In her younger days she might spend a weekend with close friends or relatives such as Lord and Lady Brabourne (she is a

---

*To put the royal accommodation in perspective, Windsor Castle is estimated to have 680 rooms, Sandringham (after some recent demolitions) about 550 and Balmoral around 250.

# BUCKINGHAM PALACE

## A general plan of the Palace's main rooms.

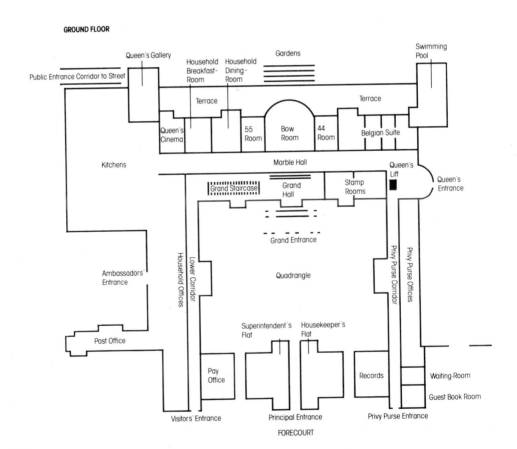

**GROUND FLOOR**

Queen's Gallery

Public Entrance Corridor to Street

Household Breakfast-Room

Household Dining-Room

Gardens

Swimming Pool

Terrace

Terrace

Queen's Cinema

55 Room

Bow Room

44 Room

Belgian Suite

Kitchens

Marble Hall

Queen's Lift

Queen's Entrance

Grand Staircase

Grand Hall

Stamp Rooms

Grand Entrance

Ambassadors' Entrance

Household Offices

Lower Corridor

Quadrangle

Privy Purse Corridor

Privy Purse Offices

Post Office

Superintendent's Flat

Housekeeper's Flat

Pay Office

Records

Waiting-Room

Guest Book Room

Visitors' Entrance

Principal Entrance

Privy Purse Entrance

FORECOURT

*106*

**PRINCIPAL FLOOR**

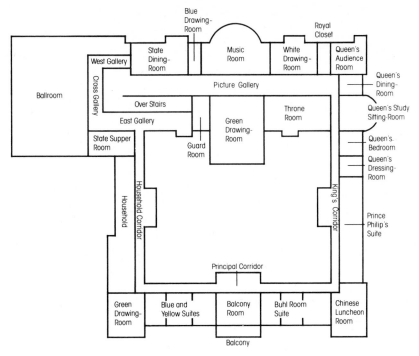

Blue Drawing-Room

Royal Closet

West Gallery

State Dining-Room

Music Room

White Drawing-Room

Queen's Audience Room

Queen's Dining-Room

Cross Gallery

Ballroom

Picture Gallery

Over Stairs

Queen's Study Sitting-Room

East Gallery

Green Drawing-Room

Throne Room

State Supper Room

Guard Room

Queen's Bedroom

Queen's Dressing-Room

Household Corridor

Household

King's Corridor

Prince Philip's Suite

Principal Corridor

Green Drawing-Room

Blue and Yellow Suites

Balcony Room

Buhl Room Suite

Chinese Luncheon Room

Balcony

**BEDROOM FLOOR**

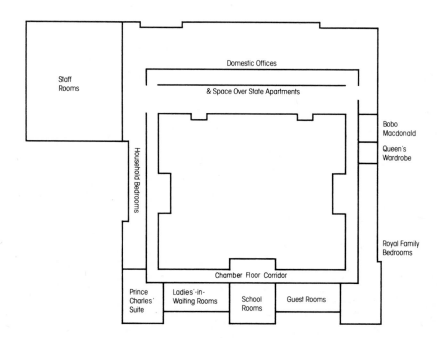

Staff Rooms

Domestic Offices

& Space Over State Apartments

Bobo Macdonald

Queen's Wardrobe

Household Bedrooms

Royal Family Bedrooms

Chamber Floor Corridor

Prince Charles' Suite

Ladies'-in-Waiting Rooms

School Rooms

Guest Rooms

Mountbatten). Now she prefers to relax with a few friends at Windsor, where she has established a restful routine, even if the air is filled with the noise of the jets landing and taking-off at nearby Heathrow. In April she likes to find time to have a longer weekend at Badminton, the palatial country house of the Dukes of Beaufort in the Cotswolds and the venue of the now prestigious Three-Day Horse Trials in which her daughter Anne, and her husband, Mark Phillips, have played a large part.

In the Palace the Queen and Prince Philip have what are virtually two large flats. On the ground floor of the north wing below them are conveniently situated the offices of the principal royal officials. On the second floor, above the main quarters of the Queen and Philip, are bedrooms and bathrooms for members of the family – Prince Andrew, Prince Edward and also for Princess Anne and her husband, who do not have a home in London. They could, of course, have one if they so wanted, but over the years Anne has grown to dislike London more and more. Subsequently when she has an engagement in town, she only stays at the Palace overnight if it is difficult to get back to Gatcombe Park, her Cotswold home.

For her routine arrivals and departures the Queen uses the secluded 'Queen's Entrance', which is at the north side of the Palace. Beyond the entrance hall is a lift built round a staircase. When the Queen steps out on the first floor, immediately in front is her Palace headquarters, the study-cum-sitting-room, identifiable on the Palace plan because it is the only room in the wing with bow windows. To the right is another sitting-room where she can relax, really putting her feet up, looking at the twenty-six-inch colour television screen, glancing at magazines, studying the form book. Around her will be some, if not all, of the pack of nine corgis. Here Philip will join her, especially in the evenings when he comes home from some public dinner he has addressed. The Queen rarely attends such functions for she finds them boring. Beyond are her bedroom, bathroom and dressing-room, which is also equipped for the coiffeur, the cosmetic artist, the manicurist. There is another room for the masseur.

To the left of the study/sitting-room is the Queen's Dining-Room where she takes her breakfast and any other meals for which she has no engagements, with Prince Philip and perhaps one or more of her children who are staying there at the time – and who are invited.

Beyond the Dining-Room, on the corner of the north and west wings is the Queen's Audience Room, where she receives the most important visitors such as the British and Commonwealth Prime Ministers in surroundings of some grandeur.

Beyond the Queen's suite on the right are Prince Philip's apartments which consist of an office, a small reference and general library in a lobby, bedroom, bathroom and a big dressing-room containing some of his clothes and uniforms together with a well-equipped corner for the almost daily visit of his hairdresser.

Directly above the Queen's apartments are the bedroom, bathroom and sitting-room of her erstwhile nurse and dresser, Mrs* Margaret Macdonald. 'Bobo' (the nickname comes from a hide-and-seek game played in the nursery) is in her late seventies (b. 1904) but determined to stay close to her 'Lillibet' (the lisping pronunciation Elizabeth gave to her own name in early childhood). Some years ago the Queen offered her one of the agreeable 'grace-and-favour' homes on the royal estates with generous financial arrangements. The offer was refused so emotionally that the matter was dropped. 'Bobo', the daughter of an Inverness farmer, has shown single-minded tenacity in retaining the intimate relationship that has developed since she first came to nurse the six-week-old Elizabeth. For twelve years or more she slept in the same room sharing the laughter, consoling the tears, watching jealously over her ward. It was inevitable that Elizabeth, a shy, somewhat introverted child, became dependent on her fond nurse, accepting almost without question her judgments on morals, people and even taste in clothes. The outlook of the Queen on life has probably been more influenced by 'Bobo' than anyone else. In a way their relationship is a secret world born of simple nursery rhymes and fairy-stories, childish fears and fantasies, overlaid with Scottish commonsense and Celtic romance. This secret world gave Elizabeth an inner confidence. It has also given 'Bobo' power.

By the time Elizabeth married, 'Bobo' was not only dresser but confidante, waking Elizabeth each morning with her cup of tea and greetings. Philip at times was justifiably annoyed at his wife's deference to her opinions which went far beyond suggestions of what clothes or jewels she should wear. He soon learned, however, that it was best to leave well alone.

Finally, when Elizabeth became Queen it was for 'Bobo', the farmer's daughter, an impossible dream come true. Her 'babe' was

---

*The 'Mrs' is the traditional courtesy title given in grand houses to senior female staff, even if unmarried.

adorned with crown and sceptre, glittering with jewels and brocade while the world paid obeisance.

For many years 'Bobo' went on all the great royal trips abroad by air and sea, provoking some jealous mockery by other members of the staff when she delivered herself of some sententious judgment employing the royal 'we' – 'No, we were not pleased with that arrangement' . . . or . . . 'Yes, we were quite delighted with the reception given us today.' The staff, however, realised that 'Bobo' was a kindly person who would intercede with the Queen in times of trouble.

'Bobo' has devoted her life to Elizabeth. She has no other interest in life other than watching over her interests. Sometimes, however, the ladies-in-waiting and the couturiers have had misgivings about 'Bobo's' influence on the Queen's clothes especially when she was younger, for it was weighted down on the side of conservatism to the point of dowdiness. Now it does not matter so much, since a more original or adventurous style of dressing would not be appropriate to the Queen in her middle years.

'Bobo's' influence in more important matters has probably also reflected a safe, cautious attitude to life. The same could not be said of another Scot, John Brown, Queen Victoria's favourite, who rose from ghillie to 'personal attendant in Scotland' to 'constant personal attendant on all occasions' and finally was officially entitled 'Esquire' with a house within the precincts of Balmoral. He died of a chill at Windsor at the comparatively young age of fifty-six, his stamina probably weakened by his over-fondness for whisky.

He was also a farmer's son, born and bred not far from Balmoral. His overdue familiarity with the Queen, his insolence to, among others, the Prince of Wales are, like his drinking, remembered. On the credit side, however, is his proven courage in protecting the Queen – on the first occasion in the grounds of Buckingham Palace on 27 February 1877, when an Irishman got to her carriage and put a pistol to her head. Brown jumped down from the rumble, seized the weapon and held the man down. That the pistol proved to be unloaded does not diminish Brown's courage. On the second occasion, at Windsor Station in 1883, the assailant's pistol was loaded. He was able to fire one shot before Brown brought him down.

Historically, kings and queens have often turned to comparatively humble men and women to seek their advice and friendship. It is a natural reaction to the fawning obsequiousness and flattery that surrounds a court. Both Victoria and now Elizabeth have found comfort and solace in the sincerity and devotion of a Highland Scot.

As a footnote to 'Bobo's' story, her sister, Ruby, was nurserymaid to Princess Margaret from 1930, the year of her birth. Ruby stayed with her, later as nurse and then dresser, for the next thirty-one years – until 1961, the year after her marriage to Lord Snowdon.

Next to 'Bobo's' suite on the second (bedroom) floor stretches the series of apartments which house a large part, but not all, of the Queen's Wardrobe. 'Bobo', having been for years the senior dresser, still has a look from time to time at this huge collection for old times' sake, but she was never in control of what has become over the years a highly-organised minor department of state, in which millions of pounds have been invested.

For her routine toilettes the Queen has a dresser and two assistants whose duties are to ensure that for every engagement the Queen emerges dressed in the clothes and accessories she has previously chosen in a state as near perfection as possible. That word 'perfection' is the key word to every public royal activity. That is what the Queen and Philip strive for and have tried to instil into their children.

For more formal occasions, such as the opening of Parliament or a State banquet which entail more elaborate toilettes, the Queen calls on a larger staff, including, if necessary, a couturier, to ensure that her appearance is faultless. On such occasions, dressed in one of the superb State gowns, embellished with great jewels, the Queen is, of necessity, enshrined in an almost Byzantine ritual. The public aspect of the Queen's life, whether here or abroad, is inevitably theatrical, but with the increasing pervasiveness of television cameras every appearance is becoming a film-set with no chance of a re-take, such as actors and actresses enjoy. Everything must be right the first time.

The Queen's Wardrobe is maintained by a staff of around half-a-dozen under the equivalent of a manageress who calls on specialists and sempstresses from the couturier – who for many years was Norman Hartnell, the creator of the coronation robes who was knighted in 1977. Then there was the brilliant Hardy Amies and now a more recent favourite, Ian Thomas, who worked with Hartnell for seventeen years. The Queen's shoes are made principally by Rayne and his craftsmen come in to keep the large collection in first-class order and suggest replacements. There are specialists for the military uniforms the Queen wears – notably at the Trooping the Colour on her official birthday. The Colour is trooped by a different regiment of the Guards Brigade each year and each regiment (Grenadier, Coldstream, Scots, Irish and Welsh) wears a uniform different in certain details – groupings of buttons etc. It may sound trivial, but a mistake can cause apoplectic fits in a mess! So the Queen has different scarlet tunics for each regiment.

In the Wardrobe are the splendid robes of the Orders of Chivalry of which the Queen is the head. The robes of the most prestigious Order, the Garter, are kept in a subsidiary Wardrobe at Windsor Castle, because all the ceremonies including the magnificent annual procession are held in and around the adjoining St George's Chapel.

The Queen holds honorary doctorates at many universities so that academic robes with hoods of varying colours and fur-trimmed borders are another section of the Wardrobe.

There are jodhpurs, riding habits, riding boots, rubber boots, raincoats and storm-proof jackets. There are rows of hats and bonnets. There are cupboards fitted with drawers for lingerie, stockings and a large stock of gloves for every occasion. The stock has to be large for it is a tradition that the gloves of royal ladies – especially the Queen – must be immaculate and often the lady-in-waiting carries a spare pair. All this is apart from the Queen's more personal clothes, such as tartan jackets, tartan skirts, twin-sets and headscarves.

Such a Wardrobe requires skilled management. The cupboards are of cedar wood, the endless drawers all numbered and indexed with their contents. There are large bound volumes in which every major item is listed in some detail. There are books of the designs prepared by the couturier for an official tour abroad with all the variations needed for different climates and occasions. There are also records of what the Queen has worn on just about every public occasion over recent years. The earlier volumes are kept in a separate library with account books and relevant comments, perhaps from the Queen herself. There are also rows of carefully-produced books, showing photographs of the Queen on occasions when her appearance has been important, here or abroad. Sometimes they are in black and white, sometimes in colour. They are carefully captioned so that if

Formal occasions such as the opening of Parliament require that the Queen's appearance be faultless. Here, accompanied by Princess Diana, the Queen is driven in the State coach to the Opening of Parliament on 3 November 1982.

the Queen asks what she was wearing in, say, Sao Paolo, ten, fifteen years ago, at a reception or dinner, the answer is readily available.

The Wardrobe has been designed to run as an efficient machine. When the Queen is advised it is time to order her clothes for the next year which may well include a visit to, say, nearby Germany or Scandinavia and also a longer tour of India and the Far East, lists are drawn up by the Wardrobe staff of what outfits might be still serviceable and what needs to be made.

After consultation with the Queen, a couturier is then given the task of making a preliminary plan. Hardy Amies is often chosen to create the outfits for the trips abroad; Ian Thomas for developing a style for the grand occasions, influenced by his Hartnell years, but now reflecting a new age.

Next, the couturier and his staff produce sketches and prepare a selection of fabrics, nearly always of pure silk, pure wool, pure cotton. There are certain fixed conditions now in a camera and television age. The colours must be bright and clear; the hats must leave the features of the face visible; the make-up must be simple and strong. All this is now routine work for those who present the Queen to the world, as routine as the uncreasable materials and the skirts that cannot be caught in a gust of wind when going up or down an aircraft gangway – or in some similar circumstance.

For the couturier the agonising moment of truth comes when he presents the sketches and choice of fabrics to the Queen and her own experts. His reputation, his financial future, can depend on the Queen's decision. Weeks, perhaps months, of work and worry can be crowned with a smile or destroyed with one of those cold, Hanoverian stares. Many years ago Hartnell told me that he never went to the Palace with the designs for a collection without fear and trepidation – and that was when he seemed to bask in the Queen's favour.

When the Queen has finally accepted the designs and fabrics, perhaps only after several meetings to discuss changes and modifications, the couturier will be in a position to make his costings and send them to the Palace for approval. There may be problems here for the Wardrobe manageress and the accountants of the Privy Purse department have to consider the budget available. The suppliers of all the varied items in the Queen's Wardrobe have learned to appreciate that there is no question of a Palace *carte blanche* when it comes to money. In case of a serious problem about costs the Keeper of the Privy Purse would put the facts to the Queen and ask for her decision.

The next step for the couturier is to obtain appointments for fittings and that can be difficult taking into account the many commitments the Queen has and her frequent absences from the Palace.

First fittings, modifications, perhaps one or two more fittings for the more elaborate dresses and gowns and then, finally, the royal acceptance!

The couturier returns to his salon. His waiting staff heave deep sighs of relief as they see him enter smiling. It is a time for champagne. Royal patronage is precious . . . as precious and as good as gold!

The Queen has a magnificent collection of furs, including sables and wild mink. She rarely wears them now, since the international campaign about twenty years ago against wearing the pelts of rare wild animals had an overwhelming social success. It had special support from Queen Juliana of the Netherlands. So the royal furs are in cold storage and it is unlikely they will ever be worn, even by the Queen's descendants.

Apart from the clothes and accessories of the Queen's Wardrobe there are two other sections of immense value and historic interest – the British and foreign decorations and the royal jewellery. The Queen is Colonel-in-Chief of over fifty regiments and corps in the British, Canadian, Australian, New Zealand and other Commonwealth armed forces. In honour of the royal connection the units over the years have presented jewelled badges or cockades, sometimes of great value, which the Queen wears on appropriate occasions. This splendid collection is eclipsed by the jewelled stars of the Orders of Chivalry and the splendour of over forty foreign orders of the highest rank. They have been presented by the Heads of State whom the Queen has visited or whom she has received as State guests at Buckingham Palace. The list is immensely impressive, ranging from the Grand Cross of the Legion of Honour of France to the Collar of the Order of the Nile of Egypt, the Collar and Grand Cordon of the Order of the Chrysanthemum of Japan and the Special Grand Cross with Star of the Order of Merit of the Federal Republic of Germany. It is worth noting, in a wry way, that the Queen has been presented with the Grand Cross of the Order of the Liberator, General San Martin, of Argentina and the Order of the Supreme Sun of Afghanistan.

The jewelled collars, stars and orders of this collection are of great intrinsic value for every state feels it honours itself in presenting gifts of the highest quality to other Heads of State. It is a form of national one-up-manship, however poor the country may be. In addition each order normally has a distinctive sash of costly silk that is a joy even to touch.

A senior official is in charge of this collection and he has a staff to keep the record volumes up to date. The official must be informed well in advance of any engagement by the Queen when it would be appropriate for her to wear one or more items from the collection in his care. For example, if she is attending an Icelandic function, it will be his responsibility to produce, polished and immaculate, the Grand Cross, with Chain, of the Order of the Falcon of Iceland with which she was presented in 1963.

When the Queen is going on a trip abroad, the task of this section is much more complicated. Insignia, orders and sashes appropriate to a series of receptions, banquets, balls, military parades in three or four countries must be listed, approved and then packed, carefully labelled, and entrusted in secure containers to a senior official who will be part of the royal entourage.

All this may seem bureaucratic, but without careful organisation by highly-skilled officials, a gaffe may be made which could cause a diplomatic incident in an important foreign or Commonwealth country. The whole business of 'honours' is an elaborate charade in many ways, but it is an accepted system of expressing friendly relations. The Queen, like her father and her Hanoverian predecessors, is a stickler for the protocol of ceremony. There is never any question of economising on staff in such a delicate area as the care and presentation of her collection of medals, badges and orders.

The items are of such value that they are generally kept locked away in their handsome presentation cases. The greatest security measures, however, have to be taken to safeguard the Queen's private collection of jewellery which is far and away the most valuable in the world, outshining in its riches even the fabulous Crown Jewels which are part of the State heritage. It is virtually

*Opposite:* The Queen receives her most important visitors, such as the British and Commonwealth Prime Ministers, in her Audience Room. She receives Mrs Thatcher in private audience once-weekly. No one else is present.

*Overleaf:* Margaret Macdonald, also known as Bobo, was the Queen's nanny and dresser as well as being her long-time friend and confidante. Here, she helps the Queen select from a fabulous collection of jewels.

Michael Frith '83

impossible to judge how much the Queen's collection is worth for in addition to the intrinsic value of each item, there is an incalculable historic value. The experts are unwilling to do more than hold up their hands in awe.

The jewels have for the most part been inherited from the collections of former Queens – Victoria, Alexandra, Mary and the Queen Mother. There have, however, been many splendid additions such as the most famous rose-coloured diamond in the world presented to the Queen by Dr John T. Williamson as a wedding present in 1947. It had been discovered in his diamond mine in Tanganyika that year. Originally weighing fifty-four carats it was cut to 23.60 and set in a brooch made as a stylised Alpine rose with five diamond petals. It is sometimes called the 'Queen Elizabeth Pink'.

The royal house of Saudi Arabia, immensely rich from oil revenues, has acquired a jewellery collection of the first order and has over the years presented the Queen with several magnificent pieces as marks of a deep friendship. This friendship has unfortunately been under some strain recently.

The Queen is kept informed of the great jewellery sales held by Christie's and Sotheby's, generally in Geneva. She is often presented as a woman of simple tastes never happy out of a headscarf and wellington boots, but in fact she takes a close interest in her jewellery collection and enjoys wearing the right pieces on the right occasion. She has available first-class expertise from Garrard's, the Crown jewellers, but has also consulted other eminent jewellers. With a

*Previous page, above:* Behind the pomp and ceremony of monarchy . . . the busy desk of Her Majesty The Queen. Assisted by her Private Secretary, Queen Elizabeth handles daily a workload that would daunt many a captain of industry.

*Previous page, below:* The Queen with her regular Trooping mare, Burmese, in the Royal Mews. The occasion: the Trooping the Colour, one of the most popular royal ceremonies.

*Opposite:* The Queen's private luncheon parties take place several times a year. The guests invited – usually about a dozen or so – are from all walks of life. A typical lunch might include Terry Duffy, trade union leader, Ian MacGregor, former Chairman of British Steel and now National Coalboard Chairman and Billy Beaumont, international rugby player.

collection of such a size as the Queen's, cleaning and re-setting are constantly under review.

The Queen has an unbelievably rich choice of jewels. For example, she has over twenty tiaras, starting with 'Granny's Tiara', given to her by Queen Mary as a wedding present. There is the Russian Fringe or Sunray which belonged to Queen Alexandra. It is in the style of a Russian peasant head-dress, but this is formed of platinum bands, heavily studded with diamonds! Alexandra had many links with Russia since her sister was Czarina and mother of Nicholas II who was to be murdered during the Russian Revolution.

Many great jewels came on the market after the Revolution, some carried out by refugees, some sold by the early Soviet governments to obtain essential supplies. Many were purchased by the great American collectors, and some by the British Royal Family.

The tiara worn by the Queen when she wants to be very, very grand indeed is made of fifteen interlocking circles of diamonds. Each circle contains a large pearl or, in another version, a magnificent emerald. If the Queen chooses the pearl version she wears the pearl-and-diamond Jubilee necklace given to Victoria. If the emeralds are chosen the ensemble is completed with a superb emerald necklace and matching earrings.

The wealth of the collection seems endless with diadems, bracelets, earrings and brooches, but the profusion of perfectly matched and graduated necklaces of pearls is breathtaking. The Queen normally wears pearls by day and is rarely seen without a double or triple row, even in a tweed skirt and twin-set. The clasp is a diamond, memorable in itself!

The most exclusive decoration is the 'Family Order', worn by royal ladies on a ribbon on the left shoulder at grand evening functions. The order, started by George IV when he came to the throne in 1820, is a small oval cameo with the portrait of the sovereign encircled by diamonds, with the royal cipher in small precious stones on the reverse. The Queen often wears two – one of her father, George VI,

The Queen wears the interchangeable tiara with the pearl drops, the Jubilee necklace, the long earrings which have a large drop pearl swinging inside a frame of diamonds, and the pearl and diamond brooch – all formerly Queen Mary's. Note also the 'Family Order' worn on the left shoulder. The Queen often wears two – as here – one of her father's, George VI, the other of her grandfather's, George V.

the other of her grandfather, George V. Her own order, showing her head and shoulders in evening dress, heavily adorned with diamonds, is worn against a deep yellow ribbon. The most recent recipient is Princess Diana. The other ladies with the order are the Queen Mother, the Princesses Anne, Margaret and Alexandra, the Duchesses of Kent and Gloucester, the Dowager Duchess of Gloucester and Princess Michael of Kent.

The Queen's wardrobe at Buckingham Palace with its superb organisation able to provide any item from the right pair of slippers to the right tiara is mirrored on a smaller scale by that of the Duke of Edinburgh. Apart from a comprehensive collection of clothes covering every activity from a court ball to deer-stalking, Prince Philip has over twenty-five uniforms which mark his rank and activity in the services ranging from Admiral of the Fleet, Field-Marshal and Marshal of the RAF. As a Knight of the Garter and Knight of the Thistle he wears from time to time the magnificent robes with their elaborate badges and gilded tassels. He has the splendid, often gold-embroidered robes, as chancellor of several universities and he has received the gowns and hoods of his many honorary doctorates here and abroad. He has medals and decorations from his service as a naval officer in the 1939–45 war and now holds over forty high orders presented to him by foreign governments.

To look after his wardrobe, Prince Philip does not have anywhere near as large a staff as his wife, but he does need skilled craftsmen – apart from his valet and two assistants – to ensure that he is turned-out perfectly for each occasion. This he rightly demands. It is a question of 'keeping up appearances'.

When a tour abroad is to be made the packing is a major operation presided over by a senior official with a group of experienced staff. The trunks are numbered, the contents listed and a loose-leaf file opened to record every detail, including what is to be worn on each day at each function (obviously a certain flexibility is built into the plan to cover sudden changes in the weather or the Queen's wishes). Packing, unpacking, repacking – it is all expert work if an immaculate appearance is to be presented at all times. In addition there are security men in charge of the jewellery chests for whom a tour is no holiday at all.

The Queen normally wears pearls by day. In this photograph, taken at Epsom in 1973, her favourite bodyguard, the late Commander Albert Perkins, can be seen to her left.

The royal wardrobe department in Buckingham Palace resembles in some ways the wardrobes of the Italian Renaissance princes, such as the Medici, when they housed jewels, precious objects, personal arms, gifts as well as clothes and accessories. For example, a signed portrait of the Queen and/or Prince Philip is a prized gift for our ambassadors, cabinet ministers, church prelates, service chiefs and the like. I have seen them placed like icons in our embassies abroad, in a position of great visibility. Such photographs are also presented to foreign ambassadors accredited to London and important visitors. Sometimes, in the case of very important personages, a warm message is inscribed by the Queen or Prince Philip. A store of these signed photographs is kept in the Palace and the size and value of the frame reflects the standing of the recipient. Part of the impedimenta of a tour abroad is a trunk of such photographs. In addition, decorations and Orders may well be included in the luggage so that the Queen can honour her hosts and those whom it is politic to please.

When Edward VII came to the throne he was delighted to inherit the Royal Victorian Order which was, as it is today, the sovereign's personal order over which the government has no control (the Garter has also reverted to the Crown this century). When King Edward was to make one of his frequent trips abroad, an ample supply of various degrees of the Victorian Order was packed so that he could honour those who had provided him with outstanding services. Hotel managers, great restaurateurs and others treasured such marks of royal esteem and have passed them down as family heirlooms.

Even today, when the Queen and Prince Philip make a tour abroad, they are accompanied by a staff of between forty-five and fifty. Of these, around half are dressers, valets and staff from the royal wardrobe department. It is a formidable number, but then showmanship is part of the royal scene. When Queen Elizabeth I died they found 5,000 of her gowns in one palace alone!

*Note concerning description of the interior of Buckingham Palace*
In recent years pictures, furniture and *objets d'art* have been increasingly put on show in the Queen's Gallery adjoining the Palace, loaned to other exhibitions or temporarily removed for cleaning or repair. They have not always been replaced in their old positions. There has also been some interchange between Buckingham Palace and Windsor Castle. On balance the Castle seems to have come off rather better than the Palace.

# Palace Splendour

## Queen Elizabeth Entertains Queen Beatrix

*I*T HAS BECOME the fashion in recent years to stress the humdrum aspects of the Queen's life – munching a lettuce leaf or two for a meal whilst kneeling down in the sitting-room mixing the dinner-bowls for the pack of corgis, at the same time intrigued by the latest episode in the life of the Archers and worried whether Diana is looking after William properly. All praiseworthy activities which link her comfortingly to the members of the Women's Institutes up and down the country, but the Queen is the Queen and though she does enjoy relaxing with simple chores and pastimes when she can, the pattern of her life sets her completely apart from ordinary people – not only here, but throughout the world. It is a fairytale life enclosed in protocol, ceremony and splendour, even on holiday.

For example, take an occasion when she receives a State visit and Buckingham Palace comes alive with magnificent uniforms, gowns and jewellery glittering under the great chandeliers of the State Apartments. Such an occasion was the recent heart-warming State visit when Queen Beatrix of the Netherlands came to London with her husband, Prince Claus, in November, 1982.*

Just before 1 pm on 16 November 1982, a procession of royal carriages, escorted by a Sovereign's Escort of the Household Cavalry, with two Standards, clip-clopped through the main gates of Buckingham Palace, across the forecourt, under the principal archway and disappeared from public view into the Quadrangle.

There the Queen's Guard of the 2nd Battalion, Scots Guards, with the Queen's Colour and accompanied by the Band of the Irish

---

*Beatrix, b. 31 January 1938, became Queen on 30 April 1980 when her mother, Juliana, abdicated in her favour, following the example of her mother, Wilhelmina, who abdicated in 1948. Beatrix married Claus von Amsberg, a German diplomat born in 1926, on 10 March 1966. They have three sons, thus breaking a long period this century when only daughters had been born in the Dutch Royal Family. For Queen Beatrix, the state visit to England was one of the most important social political events since she came to the throne.

Guards and the Pipes and Drums of the Battalion were waiting. There was a crisp order for the Royal Salute, followed by the clash of arms, the roll of drums, the dipping of the Colour as the first carriage came to a halt at the portico of the Grand Entrance where a detachment of the Household Cavalry was on duty with swords drawn in salute. Queen Elizabeth and Queen Beatrix stepped down between the scarlet-clad footmen. They stood as the national anthems of the two countries were played and then moved into the Grand Hall. They moved slowly to allow the other carriages to deposit their passengers and form part of the royal procession.

In the second carriage was Prince Claus and the Duke of Edinburgh; in the third, the Prince of Wales and the Princess, Monsieur H. van den Broek, the Dutch Minister of Foreign Affairs and the Master of the Horse, the Earl of Westmorland; in the fourth, Madame C. Bischoff van Heemskerck, Mistress of the Robes to the Dutch Queen, Monsieur P. J. H. Jonkman, Grand Master of the House of Queen Beatrix, Vice-Admiral E. Roest, Adjutant-General and Chief of the Military House of the Dutch Queen and the Marchioness of Abergavenny, one of the two Ladies of the Bedchamber to Queen Elizabeth; in the fifth carriage were the Dutch Ambassador and his wife, Madame Huydecoper, Mademoiselle F. M. de Graaff, Director of the Dutch Queen's Cabinet and Viscount Boyne, a Lord in Waiting; in the sixth sat Captain P. W. Osieck of the Royal Dutch Navy, Master of Ceremonies to Queen Beatrix, Lt-Colonel P. A. Blussé van Oud-Alblas, Master of the Dutch Royal Household, Madame H. G. Goudswaard, Lady in Waiting to Queen Beatrix and Lady Susan Hussey, Lady in Waiting to Queen Elizabeth; in the seventh carriage were Major A. Oudwater, the Dutch Aide-de-Camp, Colonel E. Spierenburg, Chief of the Security Service of the Dutch Royal House, Mr Philip Mansfield, the British Ambassador at the Hague, and his wife.

Queen Elizabeth led her guest into the Grand Hall of the Palace, and although Queen Beatrix is accustomed to a considerable degree of grandeur, the scene in front of her was dazzling in its splendour. Carpeted in crimson, like much of the Palace, the Hall is much as Nash intended – clusters of pale grey Carrara marble pillars with gilded Corinthian capitals, furnished with elegant mahogany and gold chairs with the royal cipher, large Sèvres porcelain bowls set in ormolu and massive floral displays. A bust of George IV appropriately stands above the marble mantelpiece.

Imagine all this crimson and gold as a background for the scene. Round the walls stood the élite members of 'Her Majesty's Body

Guard of the Honourable Corps of Gentlemen-at-Arms'. They wear scarlet jackets heavily ornamented with gold lace and from their tall, burnished helmets fall huge white horsehair plumes. Gloved hands rest on the hilt of their swords.

In the centre of the Hall, in due rank, the high officials of the Household wait, clad in formal dress. There was the Lord Chamberlain, Lord Maclean, the Mistress of the Robes, the Duchess of Grafton, with the Ladies and Gentlemen of the Household in Waiting.

As the two Queens made their entrance the ladies curtsied, the men inclined their heads with practised ease. The Lord Chamberlain advanced. After brief presentations the Queens, preceded by Lord Maclean, climbed the few shallow stairs to the Marble Hall, which runs the whole length of the west wing of the Palace. Here the Queen's Bodyguard of the Yeomen of the Guard stood with halberds and pikes wearing their splendid Tudor uniforms of scarlet doublets and tunics embroidered with royal emblems, elaborate black velvet head-gear and white ruffs. The procession then moved past more grey marble columns, more gold leaf and more massed flowers. The Marble Hall has, in fact, changed little since the days of Queen Victoria when she reviewed here the wounded veterans of the Crimean War and welcomed them to a feast in the Palace.

Such an event would not happen in the reign of the present Queen; such an event did not happen in the reign of her father and mother, George VI and Queen Elizabeth. That great woman Queen Mary, however, the consort of George V, had the *noblesse oblige* attitudes of Victoria, and realised that changes in society were inevitable. During the First World War she organised from the Palace the Central Committee on Women's Employment to give help and improve conditions of work. It soon became important enough to be taken over by government. She established and preserved links with the 'new' women, whose followers included revolutionaries and republicans and talked at length with them at secret meetings in the Palace about their lives and aspirations. As it turned out, she paved the way for future Labour Governments to accept and support the monarchy when they came to power. After the war she held great

*Overleaf:* On the evening of 16 November 1982, a State banquet in honour of Queen Beatrix of the Netherlands and her husband Prince Claus was held at Buckingham Palace, attended by over 150 guests.

tea-parties in the Palace, throwing open the Marble Hall, the Picture Gallery above and the State Apartments. There were hundreds of guests from many walks of life previously excluded from the Palace, such as trade unionists, actors and actresses, playwrights and authors. Queen Mary got her husband, George V, to talk to the guests (he found he enjoyed it!) whilst she and her daughter, Princess Mary, later Lady Harewood, did the honours.

It is arguable that in this present reign, the Palace has become more remote, more an enclosed world than it ever has been. In the early years of Victoria's reign, 'genteel' people were able to purchase tickets from the Lord Chamberlain's office to stand in the Grand Hall or on the Grand Staircase and watch the Queen in splendid array make her way to the Grand Entrance and enter her coach to proceed to Westminster and open Parliament.

Queen Beatrix's excellent command of English enriched her visit and made conversation with Queen Elizabeth a pleasure as they made their way along the semi-State Apartments that lead to the Belgian Suite allotted to the royal guests. All these rooms are on the ground floor of the west front and have an agreeable view across the terrace to the thirty-nine acres of gardens and lake beyond. First, there is the Bow-Room with more grey marble pillars, with gilded Ionic capitals, which enclose five tall French windows opening on to the terrace. The room is sparsely furnished, but contains in four recesses the most important pieces of Chelsea porcelain ordered by George III and Queen Charlotte. They are called The Mecklenburg-Strelitz table service, as they were intended for Charlotte's brother, ruler of that small German state.

The Bow-Room is the best known of the Palace apartments because thousands of guests at the garden-parties pass through it on their way to the lawns, having entered through the Grand Hall and Marble Hall. Next to the Bow-Room is the '1844 Room', decorated in white and gold with amber coloured pillars and a nineteenth-century Axminster carpet.

It is a charming room, but recalls Czar Nicholas I who stayed here in 1844. He was the tyrannical ruler who ruthlessly put down a Polish insurrection, and whose single-minded ambitions partially caused the Crimean War. When he stayed at the Palace, however, he was a welcome guest, as it seemed Anglo-Russian relations were on a sound basis. Queen Elizabeth and the Duke of Edinburgh find the room very agreeable and like giving private luncheon parties there. The Queen also holds meetings of the Privy Council here and gives some of her audiences. For the ambassadors 'accredited to the Court of St

James's', the room has a very special significance since it is here that they present their letters of credence and introduce their senior staff. It is a memorable moment in a diplomat's life for London – although no longer the centre of world power – is still considered a very prestigious posting.

There is a fine record of such a ceremony in the film, *Royal Family*, a joint BBC/ITV venture, which was shown a week before Charles's investiture as Prince of Wales by the Queen on 1 July 1969 at Caernarvon Castle. The Crown Equerry, Lt Col. Sir John Miller, who is in charge of the royal mews, sends a small cavalcade of elegant carriages with coachmen in royal livery to fetch the Ambassador. In this case, it was Mr Walter Annenberg of the United States, a very rich man indeed who had been given the London post, as is often the case, as a reward for political, mainly financial presidential election support.

At the Palace he and his secretaries, all immaculate in tail-coats and white-ties, are greeted by the Marshal of the Diplomatic Corps and given a briefing on the protocol, so many steps forward etc., then . . . 'Your Majesty, I have the honour . . . etc., etc.', before presenting the document from his Government appointing him.

The American secretaries line up in single file very much in military style behind their Ambassador. An official knocks discreetly at the closed doors – there is much discreet door-knocking at the Palace. 'Come in,' is presumably heard for the doors are then opened almost with a flourish. There is the Queen standing in the centre of the magnificent room. The Marshal bows slightly: 'Your Majesty . . . the Ambassador of . . .'. Mr Annenberg, in the American and republican tradition at the Court of St James's, just bends his neck, steps forward and begins: 'Your Majesty, I have the honour . . .' The Queen takes the letters and exchanges a few words. Then, royal permission having been granted, the secretaries enter and are introduced in turn by the Ambassador.

The ordeal is soon over, now is the time for royal smiles and hospitality. But such is the awe inspired by the surroundings, the uniforms, the liveries, the hushed deferential voices that even experienced old diplomatic hands find their throats going dry before the event. That is what Palace ceremony is all about!

The diplomats are probably too distraught to notice the royal paintings or the celebrated 'Negress head' clock in the room. One of her eyes shows the hour, the other the minutes. The eyelids can be closed and the pedestal contains a musical box which they say still works. Of its kind the clock is superb.

Next door to the '1844 Room' is the Caernarvon Room, the private Dining-Room of the adjoining Belgian Suite. It is named in honour of the eighteenth-century Marquess of Caernarvon who recommended George III to buy Buckingham House which was to be transformed by his son into the Palace. During the Second World War George VI established, after a difficult start, a close relationship with his Prime Minister, Winston Churchill. To replace the customary weekly audience the King began to invite him for lunch in the Caernarvon Room and thus have the opportunity to exchange views in the convivial atmosphere in which Churchill expanded. The King found the occasions so valuable that in time he invited other cabinet ministers to discuss the war news at similar lunches.

The most delightful picture in the room is, undoubtedly, the 1852 Winterhalter* of 'The Cousins: Queen Victoria and Princess Victoire, Duchesse de Nemours'. It is idealised, sentimental, but very stylish. By this time, no doubt, Queen Beatrix was glad to reach the easy chairs of the eighteenth-century room beyond. It is the main reception room of the Belgian Suite and is notable for the two splendid Zoffanys of George III and Queen Charlotte. A lighter note is given by Gainsborough's 'Diana and Acteon' which gave the artist an opportunity of painting a group of sensuous nudes which could at first glance be mistaken for the work of Renoir!

The Dutch guests had a few minutes to freshen themselves up before they went into lunch with the Queen and Prince Philip, who were accompanied by Prince Charles and Princess Diana. It was a comparatively small lunch party with Queen Beatrix, Prince Claus and the principal members of their suite, together with a few of the more important Palace officials.

It had been a long morning for the visitors. They had crossed by sea in the Royal Dutch Navy ship, *De Ruyter*.† They had been greeted at 11.30 am at Greenwich by the Prince of Wales who escorted them to the PLA barge *Royal Nore*. They proceeded with an escort to Westminster Pier where Queen Elizabeth, the Duke of Edinburgh

---

*Frans Xavier Winterhalter (1806–1873), a German portrait-painter much favoured by Victoria and Albert. It is said of him that he was the last court painter working in England who had something of the grand style of, say, Van Dyck.

†The choice of the *De Ruyter* was an example of the lively, ironic sense of humour of Queen Beatrix, which she showed later in her speeches during her visit. De Ruyter was one of the most notable Dutch admirals during the wars with Britain in the seventeenth century. After four days of battle in June, 1666, De Ruyter inflicted some 8,000 casualties on the British fleet.

and eight other members of the Royal Family were waiting to greet them with the Prime Minister, members of the Cabinet and a score or more dignitaries. There were national anthems played by the band of the Welsh Guards, a Guard of Honour to inspect whilst an artillery salute was being fired in Hyde Park.

They then set off in their carriages through streets lined with troops. The Mall was decorated with banners in the Dutch national colours, orange, white and blue, right up to the Palace. The lunchtime crowds were not large, but there were enough people to give a hearty welcome.

It was to be a long, memorable day ending with a state banquet in the Palace. Before then, however, there were other engagements for the visitors, including the ceremonial exchange of gifts witnessed by the Dutch and British courtiers. The Queen bestowed on Beatrix the Royal Victorian Chain which was instituted in 1902 by King Edward VII to be 'a pre-eminent mark of the Sovereign's esteem and affection'. (Queen Beatrix's mother, Queen Juliana, is a Lady of the Order of the Garter. No doubt in time Beatrix will be similarly honoured.) The Dutch Queen was also given two fine examples of Janet Leach pottery to add to her collection of contemporary art. Prince Claus was invested with the Grand Cross and Collar of the Royal Victorian Order and a pre-publication copy, magnificently bound, of the catalogue of Dutch paintings in the British royal collection. Thanks mainly to the Prince Regent, later George IV, this section of the royal collection is outstanding, with Rembrandts of the quality of 'The Lady With a Fan' and 'The Shipbuilder and his Wife', the Pieter de Hooch, 'The Card Players' and Jan Steen's, 'The Morning Toilet'. It was George III, however, who acquired one of the great European masterpieces for the collection, Vermeer's, 'The Music Lesson; a Lady at the Virginals with a Gentleman Listening'. It was part of the Venice collection of Consul Smith that the King bought. At the time the painting was not highly considered and certainly not attributed to Vermeer, whose genius had yet to be recognised.

Queen Beatrix and Prince Claus were also presented with photographs of the Queen and the Duke of Edinburgh in silver frames.

The return gift from Queen Beatrix was waiting outside in the gardens to be presented. 'Valentine', a brown, three year old gelding, had been chosen by experts from fifty possible candidates to be a fit gift to that very knowledgeable judge of horseflesh, Queen Elizabeth II. 'Valentine' was said to be amenable to harness and to have a very nice character so he should be an agreeable addition to the royal stables, probably at Windsor.

In the afternoon Queen Beatrix and her husband drove to Westminster Abbey to lay a wreath on the grave of the Unknown Warrior, went on to Clarence House to pay their respects to the Queen Mother and returned to the Palace to give their own reception for professors and students teaching and learning Dutch in British universities.

Before the state banquet there is time to give some details of the men and women of the Palace household who had played a part in the welcome of the guests. The description may also shed some light on the immensely complicated structure of the British court.

First, 'Her Majesty's Body Guard of the Honourable Corps of Gentlemen-at-Arms' who were on duty in the Grand Hall. This is the oldest royal bodyguard, founded by Henry VIII in 1509, the year he came to the throne, and at first entitled 'The Gentlemen Pensioners'. In the early nineteenth century William IV gave them their present grand title. There are only thirty-two of them, including a Harbinger, Standard Bearer, Clerk of the Cheque and Adjutant. They are generally former officers of considerable distinction, often of noble birth. They are proud to be the Queen's 'nearest guard' as they are the closest to the Queen, especially at all State occasions and many Palace functions. By their bearing and traditions they are a body of chosen officers who can be imagined defending the Queen on the steps of the throne with flashing swords. It is ironic to relate, however, that these gallant 'Gentlemen-at-Arms', who would fight to the last man for the Queen, were just not in a position to protect her bedroom from a wandering intruder called Michael Fagan. Such is the illusion of ceremonial bodyguards!

The Captain of the Corps is Lord Denham, who is Chief Government Whip in the House of Lords. The post is one of the few appointments to the royal household which has remained political. In the early days of Victoria's reign (1839) she created a constitutional crisis ('The Bedchamber Question') by refusing to dismiss her Whig ladies-in-waiting when the incoming Tory Prime Minister, Sir Robert Peel, quite in accordance with normal practice, wanted to replace them with women of Tory families. Victoria was a high-spirited young woman and got her own way – for the time being. Gradually, however, political appointments in the household were seen to be something of an insult to the sovereign and are now few and far between.

'The Queen's Bodyguard of the Yeomen of the Guard', who were on duty in the Marble Hall are often confused with the 'Beefeaters', the Warders of the Tower of London. This is understandable since both units wear a similar Tudor uniform. The Warders of the Tower, however, do not take part in royal events. Their task is to act as genial guides and ceremonial guard in the Tower, the oldest royal Palace, yet more renowned in history as a doom-laden prison than as a residence.

The Yeomen, on the other hand are an integral part of the royal ceremonial. They march alongside the royal coach at coronations and the annual opening of Parliament, they distribute the purses of Maundy money and attend state functions at the Palace. Like the Warders of the Tower, they are all men who have served long and honourably in the ranks of the more distinguished regiments of the Army. Their duty is to appear solid and dependable, as a foil to the aristocratic panache of the Gentlemen-at-Arms.

After the bodyguards, the courtiers.

When the Queen and her guest, Queen Beatrix, entered the Grand Hall, it was Lord Maclean, the Lord Chamberlain, who stepped forward to greet them. Many of the grand titles at the court are now honorific, but Lord Maclean does do a real job, even if it is not full-time. In person he is one of those attractive 'John Buchan' hero types to be found in the Scottish establishment. He was sixty-seven years old in May 1983, well-built, distinguished-looking, happier in the kilt, no doubt, than in his splendid court uniform and carrying his long white wand (broken on the death of the sovereign) whilst walking backward before the royal procession on State occasions. He is the twenty-seventh chief of the Clan Maclean, which is proof enough of a lineage hallowed in Celtic mists of time. He is a landowner and breeder of Highland cattle on the Isle of Mull and lives in the ancestral Duart Castle there. After war service he returned to his estates, but also devoted himself to the Scout Movement and became Chief Scout of the Commonwealth.

He is just the sort of man the Queen would want to have around, unquestioningly loyal and sound on deer-stalking. He has a grace-and-favour apartment in St James's Palace where his own department has offices. He is the highest-ranking court official and all five departments of the Palace come under him. Being the British court, it is not quite that rigid, but still by protocol, he is the boss.

The four departments other than his own are run by the Private Secretary (who is also in charge of the press section), the Keeper of the Privy Purse and Treasurer to the Queen, The Master of the Household and the Crown Equerry.

Lord Maclean, the Lord Chamberlain, is the highest ranking court official and, by protocol, head of all five departments of the Palace. He is responsible for all State and court ceremonies, except coronations and State funerals which are looked after by the Earl Marshal.

The Lord Chamberlain is responsible for all State and court ceremonies, except coronations and state funerals which are the province of the Earl Marshal (a hereditary post vested in the Dukes of Norfolk). Lord Maclean's department has to handle, for example, all the state visits of foreign Heads of State, royal weddings, investitures and garden-parties. It is responsible for the Queen's Gallery and oversees the immensely complex routine of organising the annual moves of the royal household to Balmoral and Sandringham. This work is said to have been lightened by a computer programme, but some of the older staff are terrified at the thought that the computer may forget an important item – such as Prince Philip's trews!

The chief executive of the Lord Chamberlain's department is, like so many officials at court, a former Guards officer, Lt Col. Sir Eric Penn, a Grenadier. He is a first-class staff officer, as is essential in his job, for the work in organising the events of such a State visit as we are describing is daunting. Preparations begin months in advance and entail such detail as what Queen Beatrix and Prince Claus like for breakfast and whether they would appreciate a television set in the bedroom or consider it vulgar.

There are skilled male and female staff working for Sir Eric Penn on these necessary minutiae. There are also nine lords-in-waiting attached to the department who are rather grand personages. Two of these have permanent status in honour of past services to the Queen – Lord Cobbold, previously Governor of the Bank of England, who was Lord Chamberlain before Maclean and Lord Charteris who, as Sir Martin Charteris, was private secretary until he retired in 1978 and went to Eton as Lord Provost. The other lords-in-waiting attend the Queen on a rota system.

In addition there are a score or so of Gentlemen Ushers and Extra Gentlemen Ushers, former officers, more often than not of the Guards Brigade, chosen for their distinction and bearing. They officiate at investitures, receptions and garden-parties. They all seem to be tall, slim and handsome, wearing immaculate morning-dress with grey topper and pencil-slim rolled umbrella, and they perform with effortless ease. When the Queen appears with, say, the Queen Mother, Princess Margaret and Prince Philip, the Gentlemen Ushers, toppers now in hand, escort each to a lane of guests which has miraculously appeared out of the throng. In some mysterious way certain male and female guests have been chosen to exchange a few words with royalty. And those chosen ones have somehow been ushered by the Gentlemen Ushers into the front rank of each lane. What is more, royalty seem to have been briefed on the Mayor,

Mayoress, company chairman and wife and so on with whom they are to speak.

If only, I used to think, such management skills as the Gentlemen Ushers showed had been employed in industry, our post-war history might have been different.

The patronage of Lord Maclean, whose life-peerage was granted in 1971 when he took on the Palace job, covers a very wide field indeed of court appointments. He has a shortlist of names to put to the Queen when a vacancy occurs, but often it is far from sure that any will be accepted for she has her own views about who should have the jobs and the prestige that goes with them. Among the appointments, for example, is that of the Surveyor of the Queen's Pictures, now held by Sir Oliver Millar, a position still haunted by the dark shadow of the late Anthony Blunt, the self-confessed Russian agent. The post of Master of the Queen's Music is held by the Australian composer, Malcolm Williamson. The Poet Laureate is Sir John Betjeman, who is much admired by Prince Charles. In his official capacity he produced the following lines for the wedding of Princess Anne to Captain Mark Phillips on 14 November 1973:

> 'Hundreds of birds in the air
> And millions of leaves on the pavement.
> Then the bells pealing on
> Over palace and people outside,
> All for the words "I will"
> To love's most holy enslavement –
> What can we do but rejoice
> With a triumphing bridegroom and bride.'

Mr Tom Pendry, a Labour MP, was not the only one who concluded, 'They are the words of an idle scribbler and he ought to be got rid of'.

The list of appointments is endless, but among the more glamorous are those of the Keeper of the Crown Jewels in the Tower (Major-General G. H. Mills), and the Constable of Windsor Castle (Marshal of the RAF Sir John Grandy). There is also, on another level, the Queen's Bargemaster, Mr E. Hunt, who is in charge of the Queen's Watermen, who were on duty on the Thames on the arrival of the Dutch Queen and Prince Claus. So perhaps this list of appointments can be rounded off on a Spenserian note – 'Sweet Thames! run softly, till I end my song' with the Keeper of the Swans, Mr F. J. Turk, who with his assistants rings the royal cygnets each year that 'come softly swimming down along the lee' between London Bridge and Henley.

With Lord Maclean in the Grand Hall of the Palace as Queen Elizabeth and Queen Beatrix entered was the Mistress of the Robes, the Duchess of Grafton. She was born Anne Fortune-Smith in 1920 and married in 1946 the Earl of Euston, who became by inheritance the 11th Duke of Grafton in 1970. The Duchess, whose court title is, as with so many Palace appointments, quite misleading, has nothing to do with the Queen's Wardrobe, but is the most senior of the ladies-in-waiting and appears, nobly dressed and jewelled, behind the Queen on great occasions such as the opening of Parliament, State visits and royal performances at Covent Garden.

As with Lord Maclean, she has been a friend of the Queen for many years. She was a Lady of the Bedchamber from 1953 until 1956, and has been Mistress of the Robes for the last sixteen years.

The Duchess has, as badge of office, a miniature of the Queen set in a jewelled oval brooch which is worn below the left shoulder. A golden key used to be worn by the Mistress of the Robes, but that redoubtable woman, Sarah, wife of the great John Churchill, first Duke of Marlborough, refused to give hers up when Queen Anne finally plucked up courage to sack her.

After the Mistress of the Robes rank the two Ladies of the Bedchamber. One of them, the Marchioness of Abergavenny, has already been mentioned as riding with members of the Dutch royal suite in the fourth carriage of the procession. Her husband, the Marquess, is 'Her Majesty's Representative at Ascot', and from offices in St James's Palace is responsible for deciding who may or may not enter the royal enclosure during the race-meeting. Some men and women have by birth the entrée whatever recent blots may have soiled the family escutcheon. Others of recent wealth or fame may find themselves excluded for peccadilloes. The enclosure is one of the last bastions of privileged power exercised without right of appeal or explanation.

The Marquess's brother, Lord Rupert Nevill, who died recently, had been for many years secretary and friend to Prince Philip. The list of names published in *The Times* and *Daily Telegraph* of those attending Lord Rupert's memorial service was a roll-call of the top echelon of the British establishment.

Lord Rupert and his wife, Anne, daughter of the Earl of Portsmouth, were among the very few whom the Queen and Philip would visit for the weekend, from time to time.

The second Lady of the Bedchamber is the Countess of Airlie, who is also closely connected to the Royal Family. Her husband's brother, the Earl of Airlie, is Angus Ogilvy, who married Princess Alexandra.

Ranking below the two Ladies of the Bedchamber who attend the Queen on the more important occasions, are four Women of the Bedchamber. They are from well-connected, generally rich families, but perhaps not quite so grand as the families of the 'Ladies'. The four are Dame Mary Morrison, Lady Susan Hussey, Lady Abel Smith and Mrs John Dugdale. To help out are two Extra Women of the Bedchamber, Mrs John Woodroffe and Lady Rose Baring.

Lady Abel Smith is, however, a special case, for her family is descended by marriage from a son of Queen Victoria, Prince Leopold, Duke of Albany.

The Ladies-in-Waiting have a fairly demanding job for which they are given the equivalent of a small expense account to cover the extra cost to their own wardrobes. They work two weeks at a time and when the Queen is in London they can generally manage to get home at nights to their families. When the court moves to Windsor, Balmoral or Sandringham, however, they accompany the Queen and their duties are full-time. There are the occasional 'perks' of tours abroad, but these can be tense and exhausting.

Some of the six seem to work harder than others. Lady Susan Hussey, who was in the sixth carriage of the carriage procession for Queen Beatrix, seems to be nearly always on duty. She is an Earl's daughter, married to a *Times* newspaper director, and a capable organiser. For example, she was given the task of breaking Princess Diana into the royal routine before her marriage to Prince Charles – it was not all that easy.

The Ladies-in-Waiting are called on to answer a certain type of correspondence received by the Queen – mostly letters written by children and people of all ages who write expressing loyalty and, perhaps, a request for information of some minor point of etiquette and so on. The replies to such letters are quite rightly considered important, since they are no doubt passed around among family and friends and long treasured. They are good 'public relations'.

There is always one of the 'Ladies' with the Queen at all functions she attends. Their task may seem just humdrum, looking after royal umbrellas and gloves, but they are part of the royal entourage, able to smooth over any slight difficulty that might arise and so preserve the quality of perfection aimed at. The 'Ladies' are chosen by the Queen because she likes them, but, in addition, they all have links through husbands and families with many circles of society, and are able to keep the Queen informed on many subjects – some of them highly indiscreet. It must not be thought that all the talk in the Palace is of politics, horses and dogs!

After their reception to the professors and students of Dutch, Queen Beatrix and Prince Claus may have had a little time to examine the other grand rooms of the Belgian Suite in which they were staying – the Orleans bedroom, the Spanish dressing room, another sitting-room and finally, an exquisite Regency room.

The other distinguished guests in the party, including the Dutch Foreign Minister, had also been given splendid apartments, but some distance away in the east wing – with its fine view facing up the Mall to Admiralty Arch.

The main suites for such important visitors lie on either side of the famous balcony and the room behind it. The entire wing, though it was built in the reign of Victoria, was furnished from the Brighton Pavilion and reflects the varied taste of George IV. On the left of the balcony is the Yellow Suite. The motif of the decorations in the Drawing-Room is a delicate, but joyous jasmine yellow. Beyond are bedrooms, bathrooms, a dressing-room and a writing-room, all in the Regency style. Next is the Blue Suite of sitting-room, bedrooms and bathroom. The rooms are papered in turquoise and furnished with superb English items of inlaid and painted satinwood.

On the right of the balcony is a magnificent suite furnished in the French Empire and Regency style. It is a large suite with sitting-room, writing-room, bedrooms, bathrooms and a dressing-room.

There are two other noteworthy rooms to describe on this floor of the Palace. First, the Balcony, or Centre Room – an exotically oriental room – from which the Royal Family emerge, generally on a joyous occasion, to acknowledge the greetings of great crowds massed beyond the railings of the forecourt. Prince Regent George in his time revived the dormant taste of Chinoiserie with extravagant zeal, and brought it to new heights in the Brighton Pavilion. Queen Mary appreciated much of his enthusiasm and when she found precious Chinoiserie material unused in a Palace storeroom she decided to decorate and furnish the Balcony Room in that style. She had six antique yellow silk panels set on the walls and decorated the green

*Overleaf:* A privileged view of the balcony on 29 July 1981, the wedding day of Prince Charles and Lady Diana, seen here with two of the pages. Densely packed in the background, the crowd give the royal couple their blessing. *Photograph by Patrick Lichfield.*

silk curtains of the three French windows with Chinese embroideries. The chairs and settee were re-upholstered in a dragon design. Carpet and ceiling are celadon (willow green) in tone. Between the windows are placed great set-pieces of Chinese porcelain on heavily gilded mounts.

There was so much Chinoiserie brought back from Brighton that this east wing is chock-a-block with it. An example is the Chinese Dining-Room which is on the right-hand corner adjoining the private apartments on the north wing. This 'fantastic apartment', as Victoria's favourite Prime Minister, Disraeli, called it, has been used for generations as a fairly intimate dining-room by the Royal Family. Occasionally favoured guests such as a Commonwealth president or prime minister and his wife join them for informal lunches. At most, about twenty can sit at table, but often there are not more than half-a-dozen present.

The room is a long way from the kitchens, which are at the other end of the Palace so the food was often luke-warm, but the problem has now been solved. Meals are loaded in the kitchens onto large, electrically-heated trolleys which are then put on a service lift to the basement. There the trolleys are pushed through the long corridors to another service lift at the other end of the Palace. They are then wheeled to a small room, adjoining the breakfast, luncheon or dining-room, which has hot-plates and other kitchen equipment where a chef puts the final touches to the dishes before they are served by a page (a senior servant), assisted by footmen and waiters. It is a complicated, labour-intensive system which has foiled Prince Philip, in his young reforming days, and Treasury cost-efficiency teams which are brought in from time to time.

Disraeli was right about the room. It is fantastic, full of Chinese wall-paintings and porcelain, with a huge gilt mirror over a marble chimney-piece, crimson curtains and blue walls. It is not, by any standards, a restful room designed to help the digestion.

All these visitors' suites and rooms on the first floor of the east wing open from the principal corridor, one of the great surprises of the Palace for it is more a magnificent state apartment than a corridor. It is 240 feet long, twenty feet wide and divided into three sections by tall, double glass doors. The walls at each end are of mirror glass so that the eye is dazzled by endless reflections of ten-storied pagodas of Chinese porcelain, lacquered furniture and the famous Winterhalter group of Victoria and Albert with their elder children, painted life-size in 1846.

It is now the evening of Tuesday, 16 November 1982 and time for the elaborate court ritual preceding the State banquet which is to be held at 8.30 pm in the ballroom, attended by over 150 distinguished guests. The ritual preceding such a State event in the Palace is always memorable. But this evening, when the Dutch Queen, Beatrix, and her husband, Prince Claus were to be honoured was, as our Queen Elizabeth appreciated, memorable in a very special way. This is because the House of Orange gave Britain a King, William III, son of a Stuart princess, and married to a Stuart princess, Mary, with whom he jointly and brilliantly reigned in the late seventeenth century. So this Tuesday evening was a dynastic event for the House of Windsor, one-time House of Hanover, which inherited the throne of Britain in 1714 through another Stuart princess, Elizabeth, sister of Charles I.

An occasion such as a State banquet brings to life most of the magnificent state apartments on the first, principal floor of the west wing of the Palace, those apartments conceived by Nash and his master, George IV. For the Royal Family such an evening as this begins in the Closet, which is on the far side of the west wing with the Queen's Audience-Room beyond, leading to her private apartments on the north wing.

The Closet can be called the first of the State Apartments and is not as small as its name might imply. It is an elegant Drawing-Room, with a marble chimney-piece, a graceful crystal chandelier hanging from the high ceiling, crimson damask walls on which were hung, traditionally, the Italian primitives collected by Prince Albert when they were quite under-rated and, consequently, under-priced.

The Queen certainly ensured that this evening the Royal Family was on parade in force and there they were – the men supremely elegant in evening dress with stars, sashes and miniature medals, the women in sumptuous gowns, with immaculate coiffures and glittering with tiaras, necklaces, earrings, and in some cases, stars and sashes.

Apart from the Queen and Prince Philip there was Queen Elizabeth, the Queen Mother, wearing some of her wonderful jewellery, Prince Charles and Princess Diana, Princess Anne and her husband, Captain Mark Phillips, Princess Margaret, Princess Alice, the Dowager Duchess of Gloucester, the Duke and Duchess of Gloucester, the Duke and Duchess of Kent, Prince and Princess Michael of Kent and Princess Alexandra and her husband, Angus Ogilvy. The jewellery that sparkled and glowed from a thousand facets under the chandelier would have caused envy even in the Russian court of the Romanoffs at the height of its autocratic splendour.

When the family greetings were over and, perhaps, an encouraging glass of refreshment borne on a silver salver by a page or footman, the time had come to begin the performance. It opened from the Closet with a *coup de théâtre*.

There is no door to the suite of State Apartments beyond, but when all is ready the Queen nods, a spring is touched and a sizeable part of the wall of the White Drawing-Room beyond, complete with an elaborate cabinet and huge, lofty mirror swings forward. Then in formal procession the Queen leads the way, appearing as if by magic. They say the illusion still creates an effect of awe on those not in the know. How pleased Nash would have been at his little lark!

The White Drawing-Room used to be called more appropriately the Yellow Drawing-Room for it is all gilt and grey with a set of furniture upholstered in golden yellow. The room sets the scene for the Nash grandeur to follow. The ceiling is very high with elaborate friezes. There is a great chandelier and a highly decorated piano bought by Queen Victoria at the Great Exhibition of 1851. The superb Axminster carpet of crimson and blue (forty-three feet long by twenty-five feet wide) was specially designed for the room by the same firm that created most of the others in the State Apartments.

The lasting impression of the White Drawing-Room, however, is the impact made by the first set of great twelve-foot-high double doors, panelled with mirror glass, gilded and richly ornamented. They give a brilliance of light which heightens the surrounding splendour. They are repeated throughout the State Apartments; some open to the Picture Gallery on the left; others divide the rooms, though on a ceremonial evening such as this they are left open to give a long vista of magnificence through which the royal procession makes its way.

The Queen and Prince Philip were both wearing the Sash and Grand Cross of the Order of the Netherlands Lion with which they had been presented during earlier visits to Holland. Queen Beatrix and Prince Claus repaid the compliment by wearing their British Orders. Queen Beatrix, who was then nearly forty-five, is an attractive woman with a very happy smile. She was looking her best in a simple, but elegant gown, and she wore a tiara and some splendid jewels. The Dutch Royal Family became very rich indeed from the Dutch East Indies, now independent, and prudently invested largely in Holland and America. Beatrix, however, has carried on the tradition of her mother and grandmother of avoiding ostentation, and her appearance reflected this. She was always regal, but with a touch of elegant simplicity.

The White Drawing-Room which looks towards the garden.

It is, however, in the Music Room, into which the White Drawing-Room leads, that the great ceremonial panoply of the occasion takes shape. It is a worthy setting, the most impressive and original of Nash's great State Apartments in the Palace and recalls, in the opinion of *cognoscenti*, his earlier daring at Brighton Pavilion. The Music Room is oval in shape, corresponding to the Bow-Room beneath, with a lofty, decorated, domed ceiling supported by eighteen columns of deep blue scagliola (an imitation stone of plaster), with elaborate gilded capitals. The great windows, curtained elaborately in red and gold, look out beyond a balcony to the gardens. At night the room is filled with light from two magnificent chandeliers which, like most of those in the State Apartments, came from Carlton House. The room is sparsely furnished because its rôle is to be a background for great assemblies, but the brass inlaid walnut piano was made for the Prince Regent and has been played since by musical members of the Royal Family (especially Princess Margaret), and in the last century by great virtuösi who used to be invited to the Palace. The scene is one of fairy-tale splendour.

The guests invited to the banquet had already arrived at the Palace, either through the Grand Entrance or the so-called Ambassador's Entrance on what was called, 'the Pimlico side', the south wing, in Buckingham Palace Road. The entrance is not used solely by ambassadors, but also by those with the *entrée*: Cabinet Ministers, high dignitaries and friends of the Queen whom she wishes to honour.

The Grand Staircase ascending from the ground floor to the State Apartments is very grand indeed. It is a double staircase, with a left-and-right-hand side, made of marble with heavily gilt bronze balustrading, carpeted in crimson and lit by a great domed skylight. The two sides meet at the top in a curved bow and there in front are the great gilded doors leading into the Guard Chamber with its statuary in classical style with place of honour for Prince Albert as a Roman general.

The guest has finally arrived in the halls of royal splendour.

Beyond the Guard Chamber lies the imposing Green Drawing-Room (green walls, green silk upholstery, crimson and gold carpet). This apartment is directly above the Grand Entrance and Hall and here the guests are marshalled with infinite grace, courtesy and firmness by a flock of lords-in-waiting and equerries. From the Green Drawing-Room it is only a few steps across the Picture Gallery to the Music Room where the two Queens, surrounded by family and court, greet the guests.

It is at such a time as this that the experts on protocol in the Lord Chamberlain's Office come into their own. Ordinary mortals have little appreciation of the niceties which can furrow the brows of these experts as they draw up their lists for presentation and the 'placements' at the banqueting table. Reputations can be irretrievably lost if the Right Hon. Chairman of the Greater London Council and his Lady are not given the right degree of precedence over the Lord Mayor and Lady Mayoress of Westminster.

This evening there is a great gathering of the British establishment and a fine selection of Ambassadors and High Commissioners, including His Excellency the Ambassador of the United States of America and Mrs Louis. The men wear their medals, crosses, stars and sashes if they possess them, and the women are in their most elegant gowns, wearing dazzling jewellery. Indeed there are some tiaras which rival those of the royal ladies.

The list of the Cabinet present follows the rule of precedence, not of actual power. First comes Lord Hailsham, the Lord Chancellor, followed by Mrs Thatcher, the Prime Minister. Then comes the Lord President of the Council and the Lord Privy Seal who are in front of Mr Whitelaw, the Home Secretary, and Mr Pym, the Foreign Secretary.

There follows the Archbishop of Canterbury, the Speaker of the House of Commons, the Earl Marshal, Duke of Norfolk, the Lord Chief Justice of England, the Right Hon. Michael Foot, Leader of the Opposition in the House of Commons, the Governor of the Bank of England, Rt Hon. Gordon Richardson (he had not yet received his peerage), Service Chiefs, Field Marshal Sir Edwin Bramall and Air Chief Marshal Sir Keith Williamson . . . and so on and so on.

The guests then pass on towards the ballroom where the banquet is to be held, but certain very important people are quietly requested to remain in the Music Room with the royalty. The reason is that they will be part of the royal procession which is being formed under the aegis of the Lord Chamberlain. The traditional route to the ballroom is from the Music Room through the Blue Drawing-Room, the State Dining-Room and the West Gallery.

Now all is ready. The Queen nods approval and the royal procession starts on its stately way. This was the order:

| | |
|---|---|
| THE QUEEN OF THE NETHERLANDS | THE QUEEN |
| THE PRINCE PHILIP, DUKE OF EDINBURGH | PRINCE CLAUS OF THE NETHERLANDS |
| The Prince of Wales | QUEEN ELIZABETH THE QUEEN MOTHER |
| The Archbishop of Canterbury | The Princess of Wales |
| His Excellency Monsieur H. van den Broek | The Princess Anne, Mrs Mark Phillips |
| Captain Mark Phillips | The Princess Margaret, Countess of Snowdon |
| The Lord Chancellor | Princess Alice, Duchess of Gloucester |
| The Duke of Gloucester | Her Excellency Madame C. Bischoff van Heemskerck |
| Mr Denis Thatcher | The Duchess of Gloucester |
| The Duke of Kent | The Prime Minister |
| His Excellency Monsieur P. J. H. Jonkman | The Duchess of Kent |
| Prince Michael of Kent | Princess Alexandra, the Hon. Mrs Angus Ogilvy |
| The Hon. Angus Ogilvy | Princess Michael of Kent |

This list, perfect in protocol, throws a shaft of clear light on the unchanging rigidity of the British court – and perhaps of British society in its upper reaches. Notice the high precedence of the Archbishop of Canterbury, Primate of the Church of England. Notice that Princess Diana takes precedence over the Queen's daughter, Anne, and her sister, Margaret. Notice that Mrs Margaret Thatcher, who was invested as Prime Minister with real power, comes behind not only the Lord Chancellor, but her own husband, who is in protocol appropriate as escort to the royal Duchess of Gloucester.

First on the traditional procession route is the Blue Drawing-Room which is generally considered the most beautiful of the State Apartments. It is sixty-eight feet long and was used by Victoria as a ballroom until the new one was built. The brocades on the walls, the curtains and upholstery of the elegant suites of furniture are blue, but the carpet is of crimson and gold and repeats the three gilded domes of the ceiling. The room, with four great chandeliers, is certainly magnificent and is essentially as Nash designed it, although it was not completed until 1835/36.

The State Dining-Room beyond was where Harold Nicolson dined in 1937, but he did not describe the Hanoverian family portraits which are its principal glory. Over the mantelpiece is the splendidly showy painting by Lawrence of George IV in his Garter robes, mounted in a spectacular gilt frame. It is under this portrait that the monarch presides at the Spanish mahogany dining-table which can seat sixty guests when fully extended. There are four Gainsborough portraits, including those of George IV's parents, George III and Queen Charlotte. George III is wearing the 'Windsor uniform', a blue evening coat with red facings which was de rigueur for the court when dining at the Castle. The Queen has re-introduced this costly tradition since the war.

The family record on the walls of the room goes back to a Kneller of Queen Caroline, the former Princess of Brandenburg-Anspach, who married George II.

Beyond is the West Gallery and the first vista of the ballroom decked in banqueting garb. On such a festive evening the great room (123 feet long, 60 feet wide, 45 feet high) comes to life. In the usual photographs showing a great space bare of furniture except for the thrones on the dais and the rows of crimson benches on each side, it looks rather cold and empty.

Tonight, the great room is dazzling with brilliant colour as the royal procession make its stately entrance. The six great rose chandeliers light up a fantasy world of crimson, gold and white. As Queen Elizabeth invites Queen Beatrix to enter, the string band of the Welsh Guards up in the Musicians' Gallery at the far, far end of the room strike up the Dutch and British National Anthems.

The Queen leads her royal guests to places of honour beside her at the top table which on such occasions is placed in front of the throne dais against an almost overwhelming background of red hangings made from the draperies of the Imperial Shamiana under which George V and Queen Mary were enthroned at the Delhi Coronation Durbar of 1911.

In front of the royalty the banqueting tables are set in horseshoe

155

A view of the Throne Room from the Green Drawing-Room. The two mirror doors on the left lead into the Picture Gallery. There is, strictly speaking, only one throne and that is in the Palace of Westminster.

fashion. The glossy damask cloths have been laid by the team of expert 'table-deckers' whose task is also to arrange the silver, the centre pieces, the table bouquets, and the wine glasses which are issued by the Yeoman of the Glass Pantry. 'Pantry' in these titles means a strongroom with every item issued and returned against signature by a senior official. The massive flower displays round the room and throughout the Palace are the responsibility of another team – the florists who with years of training and devotion have set almost incomparable standards.

Along the side walls, in all its glory, the State Gold Plate has been arranged beneath the tapestry panels under the supervision of the Yeoman of the Gold Pantry for whom such an evening is a proud occasion as it is, indeed, for his colleague, the Yeoman of the Silver Pantry.

The parquet flooring of the ballroom has been covered with red carpet, giving more warmth of colour to the huge room and also ensuring almost silent service by the footmen, resplendent in scarlet and gold livery with white breeches, stockings and buckled shoes. On these occasions they no longer, as in previous reigns, have to powder their heads with a mixture of flour, starch and soap. In his early reforming zeal and fresh from war service, Prince Philip convinced the Queen that this was too redolent of 'ancien régime'.

To add yet another note of grandeur to the occasion, the Yeomen of the Guard are on duty again, this time spaced around the walls in their elaborate scarlet, Tudor uniforms. The Steward of the Household, a senior personage, is also on duty on such occasions, watching with eagle-eye at a convenient vantage point to ensure that everything goes without a hitch, especially at the top table.

Royalty is now seated. Lesser mortals take their places. At a nod the first course of the banquet is served with magic efficiency by scores of white-gloved hands. From the serving tables comes a soup, Crème Solferino, and a sherry, 'Fine Old Amontillado' – the first of the wines which have been brought up by the Yeomen of the Wine Cellars. As royalty, nobility and dignitaries begin to sip, the string band encourages a festive spirit with 'Colonel Bogey' and a selection from Novello's 'Perchance to Dream'. The next course is Coquilles St Jacques Mornay, a classical concoction of cockles with a superb sauce. The wine to accompany it is a Mosel, Trierer St Maximiner Kreuzberg Spätlese, 1979. The Welsh Guards band continues its programme with 'The Little Swiss Polka' and a waltz selection, 'Flights of Fancy'.

Now it is time for the main dish, 'Faisan Farci Souvaroff', pheasant with a delicate stuffing, which is accompanied by potatoes, braised endives and haricots verts. From the Palace cellars is served a noble burgundy, Nuits St Georges Les Pruliers, 1969.

The pheasants are as likely as not to have been shot over the Sandringham estate by Prince Philip with the help of some family and friends. He enjoys the shoots, but the bags also make money and he prides himself that the royal estates are run profitably. Balmoral, for example, provides grouse, venison and game-fish not only for the royal table, but for sale.

The band is progressing from 'Country Gardens' by Grainger to a selection from Mary Poppins and a 'Westminster Waltz'.

By this time the scene in the vast room is spectacular. This is the world of privileged luxury that George IV, soon after the Napoleonic Wars, had visualised for himself and his Court in the new Palace Nash was building for him. Now in 1982, over 150 years later, his descendant, Queen Elizabeth II, presides over this brilliant scene in a world bristling with weapons infinitely more dangerous than either Napoleon or Wellington could have imagined at the Battle of Waterloo.

On such an evening in the Palace no musical programme could omit Gilbert and Sullivan and sure enough, around now, the band begins a selection from *HMS Pinafore*.

A salad is served at this stage to freshen the palate before the champagne, a Pol Roger 1969, and then an ice-cream dish. With champagne it is time for music with a sparkle. A 'Neapolitan Serenade' and 'The Princess of Wales' is played in honour of Princess Diana, eyes and jewels shining at the top table.

Now there is port, Dow 1966, with which to drink the toasts proposed by Queen Elizabeth to her guests and by Queen Beatrix to her hosts. Speeches by constitutional monarchs on such ceremonial occasions are, generally, gracious and brief. Queen Elizabeth, after recalling that the Bank of England had been established with Dutch finance and modelled on the Bank of Amsterdam, added: 'On a lighter plane, what Englishman has not grown Dutch bulbs, not tasted Dutch cheese and is not an expert on the technology for filling holes in dykes?' This was greeted with responsive laughter. After the speeches and applause, there are a few minutes more of animated conversation whilst the decanters of port are passed around again. Then there is a stirring among 'The Ladies and Gentlemen of the Household in Waiting' who have been in attendance. Royalty rise from their seats and all follow suit. Often at the end of a State banquet, the Queen leads the way down the ballroom, enabling all the guests to see the royal procession. Then they proceed through the East Gallery and the Silk Tapestry Room to the Picture Gallery where great paintings and furniture can be admired. This route finally leads to the private apartments with bathrooms and toilets in plenty.

Coffee and drinks are then served in the sitting-rooms. Royalty on its return receives favoured guests who are shepherded to the presence by court officials. The Queen, however, has not yet exhausted the programme of festivities arranged for her guests this evening. Her addiction to the bagpipe is well-known, if not notorious. The world has long been aware that every morning, under her bedroom windows, in whichever of her palaces she happens to be, a Pipe Major of a Highland regiment parades up and down playing for Her Majesty's pleasure and the scarcely concealed anguish of many of her nearest and dearest. It is said that the Queen

The State Dining-Room which looks towards the Ballroom.

159

is only carrying on a tradition established by Victoria, but there are doubts about this.

So this evening, as the string band of the Welsh Guards complete their programme, the Pipers of the 2nd Battalion, Scots Guards, under the direction of Pipe Major J. Riddell, all magnificent in dress kilt and tunics, expand their cheeks and begin with a march, 'The Crags of Tumbledown Mountain', followed by a strathspey, 'The Rose Among the Heather'. Then comes a lively reel, 'Thomson's Dirk' and finally a march, 'Roy Cove'.

The great evening is now drawing to a close. There are curtsies by the ladies, inclinations of the head by the men and royalty makes its way to its apartments. The guests queue for their wraps and coats and make their way out to the forecourt and surrounding streets where their cars are waiting and squads of helpful police are much in evidence.

The Ladies and Gentlemen of the Household possibly partake of a relaxing nightcap after the rigours of their duties, and exchange tales of the inevitable contretemps that occur on a big social occasion. The staff will be cleaning up for some time yet before they are free to go to their bedrooms, mainly on the attic floor of the east wing. In Prince Albert's early days at the Palace he had been angered to learn that staff took the candle-ends (often quite large) as perks at the end of a grand evening and sold them locally for a good price the next day!

## 'THE HOTEL MANAGER'

The Lord Chamberlain and his aides are in charge of the elaborate ceremonial for a great occasion like a State banquet, but the chores are the responsibility of the Master of the Household who controls the largest proportion of the Palace staff. He is Vice-Admiral Sir Peter Ashmore, not a member of one of the 'in' court families, but a distinguished officer who has done a stint as Chief of Allied Staff at NATO headquarters, Southern Europe – one of those frustrating jobs where most of your time is spent calming down outbreaks of national pique. It was, however, good training for his present position where he has to deal with the daily problems inherent in a complicated and somewhat introverted court.

It is a job that needs much patience and calm. If, for example, the Queen and/or Prince Philip have a complaint about the food, wine, or service at a banquet, it is Sir Peter who would carry the can next morning when he would be summoned to the presence.

He may be a Vice-Admiral and have high position in the Household, but this is, in fact, a workaday job with pitfalls waiting in every grand corridor. He has a ceremonial boss, the Lord Steward of the Household, at present the Duke of Northumberland, but he only makes decorative appearances on grand occasions. Nearer at home, the Lord Chamberlain also counts as senior to Sir Peter and can put his oar in.

The Admiral works from a large office on the principal (first) floor of the south 'Pimlico' wing overlooking Buckingham Palace Road. This is mainly a service and staff wing with offices on the ground floor where clerks and secretaries deal with the day-to-day tasks of keeping the Palace running smoothly. In some ways running the Palace is like being in charge of a luxury hotel and Sir Peter is sometimes called, slightly mockingly, by the grandees, 'the hotel manager'. I think he might often feel that running Claridge's would be a simple job compared with the Palace – at least in a hotel the manager is the boss!

Earlier I wrote that there were 300 full-time and 120 part-time employees in the Palace. It is as accurate a figure as possible, although it is as difficult to be precise on the subject as it is to give the strength of a battalion on any one day or the total employed in, say, the Treasury in any one year. Mr Ronald Allison, a former press secretary at the Palace, in the course of an agreeable television series on the Royal Family in spring 1983, said 350 people worked in the Palace, with extra help brought in for the big occasions. Another source, which I have learned greatly to respect, writes of 337 full-time and 126 part-time employees. So I have, in fact, opted for a fairly conservative figure to obviate criticism of exaggerating.

On balance, I think all Palace departments in recent years have tried to cut down, but neither the Queen nor Prince Philip wish to see men and women who have given good service thrown into unemployment at a time of economic recession. They know forced redundancies on a large scale would not do the royal public relations any good if the news became public – as it most likely would. Several grades of staff have for some years been unionised and relations have, if anything, improved.

Sir Peter is responsible for about 200 of the staff. He has a deputy who is ranked among 'the Household'. Peter Townsend, for example, once had the job. Under him comes a Palace Superintendent (domestic administration, with Chief Clerk and assistants), then the Steward (indoor menservants) and a Housekeeper (female staff). The Yeomen of the Gold, Silver and

Glass Pantries, and of the Wine Cellars have already been mentioned. In the kitchens are a head chef, three assistant chefs, three staff chefs and forty other workers, who would be augmented on a great occasion such as a State banquet.

To these must be added under-butlers, pages (the most prestigious is the Page of the Backstairs, who is the Queen's personal servant), then footmen and lower-grade staff waiters. Then there are the Queen's dressers and Prince Philip's valets, not an easy class to deal with for they soon come to consider themselves as 'special cases'.

There are between thirty-five and forty maids and another dozen or so cleaners, many of them with special skills in looking after valuable objects and carpets. There are teams of upholsterers, plumbers, electricians, carpenters and window-cleaners who work full-time, but live at home. The two men who look after the 300 or more clocks always attract interest. Their job is not, however, just to wind them up, as seems to be widely thought. They are craftsmen caring for a superb collection of often complicated timepieces, many of them acquired by George III.

An insoluble problem for Sir Peter when he comes to analyse the total of employees in his organisation chart, (for I am sure as a good staff officer, he does,) is that in the hierarchy of a court, class distinctions are so rigid, many of the staff spend their time looking after other staff in higher grades. The kitchens, for example, have to provide for what are virtually six 'eateries' ranging from royal dining-rooms to canteens for the kitchenmaids. The resulting economic wastage is inevitable because that is the way the court is established at the Palace and it is almost impervious to change.

Here are a few examples.

The central archway of the east wing, unimpressive as it is, is nevertheless the ceremonial 'principal entrance' to the Palace. It is flanked on the left by the commodious flat of the Palace Superintendent, and on the right by the equally commodious flat of the Palace Housekeeper. Both can, and do, call on staff to provide service. Then there is the style of living of 'the Household', the senior officials at the Palace, of whom Sir Peter is one.

Going back to the Bow-Room in the centre of the west wing of the ground floor there is on the left a series of splendid rooms, with the Nash decorations almost unaltered, for the use of 'the Household'. The view from them is delightful as the long windows open on to terrace, balustrade and gardens.

The first is the '55 Room' which commemorates the visit in 1855, of Napoleon III and his Empress Eugénie, whose voluptuous beauty in

This is Guest Bedroom No. 236. It is on the east front overlooking the
Victoria Memorial.

163

the Spanish style captivated Victoria. France was Britain's ally in the Crimean War which was being waged at the time and in this room a Council was held on 20 April 1855, attended by Queen Victoria, Prince Albert and the French Emperor to plan further operations in the campaign.

To recall the event a full-length portrait of Napoleon III and Eugénie traditionally hangs in the room. The somewhat bizarre royal friendship is further remembered by a picture of Victoria at the tomb of the great Napoleon in the Invalides during a reciprocal visit paid to Paris later in the year.

This is now the drawing-room for the Ladies and Gentlemen of the Household and the two other apartments in the suite are the Household Dining-Room and the Household Breakfast-Room. They are furnished with excellent pieces and on the walls are paintings of quality and anecdotal interest.

This graceful section of the Palace naturally plays a special part in the life of the Ladies and Gentlemen of the Household. It even envelops at times the Bow-Room itself, for it is a tradition that they gather there to bid a courtly Bon Voyage when the Queen and Prince Philip are about to leave on an important tour abroad.

All this elegant, even luxurious ambiance costs money. Breakfast, lunch and dinner are served in the style of a grand country-house that can still afford skilled servants to serve first-class food and drink. Also, from time to time there are guests chosen from social circles where the men and women might have information helpful to the Household or, on the other hand, might be used to pass on elsewhere information helpful to royalty. The network of the court is extensive and subtly maintained.

For the Ladies and Gentlemen, accommodation is also provided if their duties call for it. There are bedrooms and bathrooms for the Ladies-in-Waiting on the bedroom floor of the east wing. Similar accommodation for the men is in the south wing on the same floor. They are not provided with individual ladies' maids or valets, but there are enough personal servants made available to look after them.

More staff, more expense for the Master of the Household!

The grand ones of the Household are, however, only the tip of the iceberg. There are comptrollers, accountants, chief clerks, secretaries male and female of various grades – they all have to be looked after according to their social status even if they only work office hours in the Palace.

Sir Peter is also responsible for the communication system. There are eight or more highly experienced male telephone operators. In these days when it has become difficult to get an answer when telephoning almost any organisation, it remains normal to receive a swift, courteous response from the Palace switchboard. A Palace operator has to learn the tact of a diplomat. There are over 300 telephones and extensions in the Palace and engineers are always also at work there, just as they would be in the headquarters of a large business.

The Palace post office, another of Sir Peter's responsibilities, is rather special. It is run by a court postmaster with a staff of clerks and postmen, and now in these days of letter bombs, one or two trained security men.

The mail arrives about 7.30 am in a post office van which drives across the forecourt and is unloaded by the Palace postal staff. Sorting is mainly a routine matter and any difficulties are dealt with by the postmaster who has great experience. Deliveries are then made to the various departments, in the same way they would be made in a government department or large business headquarters. In the afternoon another van collects the mail for despatch from the other royal establishments in London (Clarence House, St James's Palace, Kensington) and delivers it to the Palace post office. There it is added to the Buckingham Palace mail and it is all despatched without charge. The royal frank is enough – on the principle that all mail, nationally, is sent by 'royal mail' so the service is the Queen's prerogative. It is a reminder that her head appears on all postage stamps, even if in miniature on special issues. An account of the expenditure is, however, kept.

The Palace post office is kept busy dealing with over 75,000 items a year.

By now it will seem that Sir Peter Ashmore's department covers just about everything from the kitchen sinks. But there is still more to come. At the trade gates on the Pimlico wing, lorries marked 'E II Royal Farms' arrive at 8 am from Windsor with milk, fruit, flowers and vegetables. Soon after there is nearly always a Harrods delivery van full of special goods. Loaves and rolls arrive from the Lyons bakeries. So it goes on most of the morning, keeping the storemen and kitchen clerks busy.

The Master of the Household is also a publisher. He is responsible for the daily 'Court Circular' which records the official engagements of the Royal Family with meticulous precision. Both *The Times* and the *Daily Telegraph* reprint it under the royal coat-of-arms in a traditional position of dignified prominence. The circular reports the activities according to strict protocol. It normally starts with Buckingham Palace, but moves to Windsor, Balmoral or elsewhere with the court. There follow announcements from, for example, Clarence House (the Queen Mother), Kensington Palace (the Prince and Princess of Wales, Princess Margaret and several other royal households there) and when appropriate also from Thatched House Lodge on the outskirts of Richmond Park (Princess Alexandra).

It looks a simple enough publication to an outsider. Any journalist, however, who has had to gather reports from various sources (often by telephone), put them together, get them printed and check the proofs will know that the Court Circular is no easy task. It must be a nightmare at times to ensure that the names and titles of the many foreign dignitaries mentioned are absolutely correct. A mistake in the Court Circular could cause a rebuke from royalty itself or a pained complaint from a ministry or embassy.

There has been talk at times that it would be appropriate if the Court Circular was produced by the Press Secretary's department which has grown in size and importance in recent years. I can well understand the Press Secretary preferring to leave it with the Master of the Household. It is a daily chore, more likely to draw brickbats than bouquets.

The police, whose duty is to guard the Palace, have a duty office on the ground floor of the Pimlico wing not far from the kitchens. It is Sir Peter's responsibility to see that the Palace is properly guarded, but his powers are so hedged in that it is a case of 'responsibility without power'. The problem of security in the Palace since the Fagan incidents needs to be examined in a wider context.

The Palace official who organises the royal transport arrangements in this country is the Crown Equerry, Lt Col. Sir John Miller, and he now deserves attention as head of another important department of the Household.

It is, perhaps, symbolic of the court that the Crown Equerry, who had had the work of organising the imposing carriage procession to the Palace on the arrival of the Dutch Queen, came at the tail-end, not in a carriage, but in a car. Meanwhile, up near the front riding with the Prince and Princess of Wales, was the Crown Equerry's boss, the Earl of Westmorland, wearing a gorgeous uniform as Master of the Horse. The position, in its day politically powerful, is now ceremonial, but it still has a special significance for the Queen and the aristocracy to whom the horse is nearly as important a status symbol as it was to the Norman conquerors. Lord Westmorland

The Crown Equerry, Lt Col. Sir John Miller, is the working manager of the Royal Mews.

belongs to the inner circle surrounding the Queen, as did and does his predecessor, the Duke of Beaufort, who even now is called 'the Master' in hunting circles. This is not a reference to his former position at court, but to his lifelong, unrelenting pursuit of the fox.

Sir John Miller, though as Crown Equerry is the working manager of the Royal Mews, has the socially correct background of Eton, Guards, polo and foxhunting (he persuaded Prince Charles to take it up). His staff consists of a Royal Mews Superintendent, a Comptroller of Stores, a Chief Clerk and around forty grooms, coachmen and postillions. There are a dozen chauffeurs of quite remarkable skill. In addition, Sir John is responsible for the ten gardeners, working under the highly professional head gardener, who is, of course, like all good head gardeners, a law unto himself. The hundred or so maintenance workers responsible to the Department of the Environment also come under the Crown Equerry when at work in the Palace and grounds.

The Royal Mews were designed by Nash and the entrance in Buckingham Palace Road through a Doric archway with a clock tower above has more than a touch of his elegance. It leads to a quadrangle with stabling for thirty or more horses, cover for over sixty carriages from Town Landaus to the historic State Coach and a comprehensive display of bits, snaffles, collars, reins and other trappings in perfect order. It is intended to be a working showplace, and is open to the public on Wednesday and Thursday afternoons, except during Ascot week. Beyond is the great covered riding school which was built for George III by Nash in the days of 'The Queen's House'. During the 1914–18 war George V and Queen Mary used to give hospitality there for large parties of soldiers, especially for those from the Empire.

There are around twenty motor cars, many of them Rolls-Royces specially designed with very large windows and raised upholstery to give the public a good view of royalty on display. Pride of place goes to the £60,000 Phantom Six Rolls-Royce presented to the Queen as a Silver Jubilee gift in 1977. The 3.5-litre Rover the Queen drives herself, generally down to Windsor on Friday afternoons, is not so much in use these days. Security has, rightly, become much more stringent.

The fleet of Rolls-Royces carry no licence plates, but have a small coat-of-arms on a roof plaque in front. Sometimes it is discreetly covered; sometimes illuminated.

Sir John is one of those men who manage to achieve a degree of perfection with a casual air that is traditionally supposed to be the hallmark of an Etonian. As Crown Equerry he has certainly maintained standards and has, consequently, to be very demanding at times.

# Royal Workaday

*A*FTER THE lavish splendour of a State visit, it is essential to describe the day to day aspects of royal life in the Palace.

Take Prince Philip, for example, spending a morning in his study/office, not far from the Queen's, on the first-floor of the north wing and determined to catch up on his paperwork. Over the years he has done his best to change the high-ceilinged, Victorian-style room into a modern office, but has only partially succeeded. He had a false ceiling installed, and a large desk and surrounds of utilitarian design. The wall-covering is a neutral grey, the carpet plain blue. The easy-chairs are modern and covered plainly. In addition to telephone and intercom there is a radio, a television set, a word-processor and other communication aids including a tape-recorder often used to make first drafts of his speeches.

The Palace atmosphere, however, is not that easily eliminated. A chandelier still hangs down through the false ceiling and attracts more attention than the modern adjustable desk-lamp. What is more, even though one side of Prince Philip may have wanted to create the office of a businessman, another side is apparent on his desk for there are several framed photographs of family which lend some grace and soften the austere simplicity.

There is no doubt, however, that his office is one of the busiest in the Palace with an official private secretary and treasurer to look after his Civil List allowance which for 1983 was £179,300, a rather overworked team of manager and five secretaries. He is patron of nearly 400 associations of which over seventy are connected with the sea. There is a mail of several hundred letters a week, some of which can be dealt with in a routine or formal way, many others Prince Philip considers carefully himself and writes out a reply in longhand which is then sent down to the office below to be typed. Many of his speeches now come easily, but if he feels the occasion warrants it, he will take a long time writing an address and correct several drafts before he is satisfied. Although he has been criticised over the years for expressing his views fully and frankly, he has also won respect for his intelligence and honesty of purpose.

His programme has to be organised nearly six months in advance and has to take into account the many occasions, here and abroad, when he will be accompanying the Queen. Then there are recurring engagements which arise from his high ranks in the services, his interest in education and industry, with emphasis on new technology and, one of his greatest achievements, the Duke of Edinburgh's Award Scheme. Whenever he can, however, he will branch out into something new which he feels his presence will encourage.

Prince Philip had to give up his career in the Navy soon after he married Elizabeth. When she came to the throne, he found himself frustrated – as Albert had been before him – at his lack of purposeful activity. The Duke, however, gradually made a niche for himself in the life of the nation, a niche that has now become a sizeable slice.

Prince Philip would probably put aside the morning for office work, which might be followed by an informal lunch. Since 1956, with his help, the Queen has been giving four or five luncheons a year for six or eight men and women who have made a mark in their careers. Whoever had the initial idea, it has proved of considerable value. An invitation to lunch at the Palace is a highly-regarded honour and the event is long-remembered and talked about for years. It has also been valuable for the Queen and Prince Philip, for over the years they have met at these lunches many men and women of talent, sometimes great talent, and although some of the guests remain over-awed and tongue-tied, others respond to the easy charm of the Queen and Prince Philip and express themselves with a certain freedom on their views on life.

Here, for example, is the guest list for the lunch given on 4 May 1983: Miss Jocelyn Barrow, lecturer, Institute of Education, London University; Sir Terence Conran, chairman, Habitat Mothercare; Mr Peter Hicks, sculptor; Lord Justice Kerr, Lord Justice of Appeal; Canon Malcolm Menin, Rural Dean of Norwich (East); Professor Graham Smith, Astronomer Royal; Mr Donald Telford, editor, *The Observer*; Mr Leslie Wood, general secretary, Union of Construction, Allied Trades and Technicians.

The guests generally gather in the Bow-Room on the ground floor and the imminent arrival of the Queen is heralded by a few of the corgis. After the guests have been introduced to the Queen and Prince Philip by an official of the private secretary's office, the way is led into lunch which is often held in the '44 Room' which leads off on the right or the Caernarvon Room beyond. The Queen and Prince Philip sit opposite each other to promote a general conversation.

The menu of the three-course lunch is simple, designed to satisfy most tastes. Beer or wine is served. The Queen always drinks alcohol sparingly and at lunchtime generally has a glass of Malvern, her favourite spa water, supplies of which follow her round the world on her trips. By all accounts the Queen is always in sparkling form at these lunches, determined to show that she is a lively, amusing woman when freed of the necessity to be politely formal.

The lunches are, by Palace protocol, 'informal' so they are not reported in the Court Circular. The names of the guests and their jobs, however, are issued through the press secretary's office and printed in *The Times* and the *Daily Telegraph*, near the Court Circular, but not as part of it.

When the Queen produces her handbag and lays it on the table, it is a sign the lunch has come to an end.

As the Queen resumes her day's work, Prince Philip may make for the helicopter of the Queen's Flight waiting on the garden lawn to take him to his next engagement. What is more he may have had to make a quick change into a uniform for he might well be attending a Naval, Army or Air Force event, at Portsmouth, Sandhurst, Cranwell, or elsewhere. Soon after 6 pm his helicopter might well deposit him back on the Palace lawn. Now he might feel the need for a refreshing splash in the swimming pool which lies on the right of the Palace near the private apartments. It is a fine heated pool, situated inside one of the old graceful conservatories and was constructed not, as many think, in this reign, but before the war by George VI. Indeed, it was damaged during one of the air-raids. Prince Philip uses it, so did Prince Charles before he moved to Kensington Palace. The courtiers of the household are also allowed to have a dip there. The occasion is still remembered, however, when Prince Andrew in his 'jokey' days before joining the Navy, having climbed up to the roofs and wrecked the Palace television aerials, later turned his attention to the pool. As a result of his scientific activities the waters foamed well beyond the surface, reaching for the ceiling and threatening to seep out of the doors. His parents were not amused! Nevertheless, though Andrew may be 'the wild card' in the pack, as a helicopter pilot during the Falkland campaign he turned up trumps!

Prince Philip now rarely visits the squash court in the basement which he made use of regularly in his early years. There was one historic moment there. On Sunday, 14 November 1948, he was in a somewhat tense mood and decided to play a game of squash with Michael Parker, the Australian naval officer who was his equerry and probably as close a friend as he has ever had. They were halfway through a game when the news arrived – Elizabeth had given birth to a healthy boy. Philip raced upstairs to the nursery which had been converted into a delivery room. The King shook him by the hand and the Queen gave him a kiss. Elizabeth was soon to see her husband standing by her bedside with a huge bouquet of roses and carnations, her favourite flowers.

To return to Prince Philip's day, after his return by helicopter it is fitting to round it off with one of the Palace dinners he gives from time to time for around a dozen or so bankers, industrialists, scientists and others whose knowledge and experience might help the economic development of the nation. These occasions are off-the-record and, at their best, result in a free-ranging discussion which can lead to practical results. The Queen does not attend, but the Prince of Wales is generally there if he is not out of town. One of the most valued members of the circle was Lord Mountbatten, whose murder in Ireland on Bank Holiday Monday, 27 August 1979, together with other members of his family, came as a grievous blow to the Royal Family.

Mountbatten, 'Uncle Dickie', had become over the years the elder statesman of the Royal Family. His influence was not so much on his nephew, Prince Philip, but on the Queen and Prince Charles. For the Queen, Mountbatten was an unofficial trusted counsellor who could draw on a boundless wealth of experience and express his views with inimitable charm as he sat tête-à-tête over dinner with her at the Palace, often as frequently as once a week when they were both in London. For Prince Charles, Mountbatten was as much a racy friend as a great-uncle. Charles could relax with him, maybe discuss his latest girlfriend (before his marriage, of course!) or exchange some piece of naval gossip or history. They enjoyed being with each other and at times were seen at the end of an evening, well 'lit-up'.

It was Mountbatten who had spotted the potential of Philip Moore at the Ministry of Defence where he was Chief of Public Relations in

A young Mr Philip Moore, photographed in December 1966, the year of his appointment as Assistant Private Secretary to the Queen; and more recently (*inset*) as Private Secretary and Keeper of the Queen's Archives – a position he has held since 1978. He is certainly the most important of all the officials at court.

1965 at the age of forty-four. Within a year, Moore was at the Palace as assistant private secretary to the Queen and in 1972 deputy private secretary. He was thus number two to Sir Martin Charteris, who retired in 1978 with a life-peerage to become Provost of Eton. Moore (now Sir Philip) then became 'Private Secretary to the Queen and Keeper of the Queen's Archives' and as such by far the most significant official of the Queen's court. He is also the man in just about daily touch with the sovereign.

For example, take any morning when the Queen is in the Palace. When she has bathed and dressed she has already opened a few personal letters and looked at the card detailing her day's engagements, before going along the corridor to breakfast at around 8.45 am in the private Dining-Room (a choice of eggs, bacon, sausages and kippers on the hot-plate, but she may settle for tea, toast and marmalade). The newspapers are all there and she will pick and choose according to her fancy and the headline displays. The racing newspaper, *The Sporting Life*, is, however, for expert appraisal, especially during the 'flat' season when she has horses running or there is a big race. If there is a crisis, home or abroad, the radio news will be turned on. The quarter of an hour of bagpipes form part of an accepted background as she sifts in her experienced, worldly-wise mind what is going on in the world. Unless the weather is very bad she likes then to have a walk in the gardens with the corgis as far as the lake and the flamingoes. The head gardener may be around and be asked why a shrub or tree she wanted to be planted is still not visible. But as she has admitted, ruefully, she doesn't always get her own way in the gardens.

It is around 10.15 am by now and the routine is for the Queen to go to her study/sitting-room and start work. The walls and curtains are blue-green, the large desk is by the long windows and presents a rather cluttered-up appearance with a gallery of handsomely framed photographs of family, dogs and horses. Her mahogany chair is big and comfortable with wide elbows. With its lofty ceiling surrounded with gold-leaf, the varied colours of the paintings on the walls, the Chinese green carpet and the displays of marvellous flowers it is a bright room, feminine enough, but grand enough without being fussy or overpowering. The corgis are sometimes, but not always, around.

When the Queen asks Sir Philip on the intercom to come up, he gathers his papers together, and probably takes with him one of the famous red boxes marked 'The Queen' which has arrived from Whitehall. The 'boxes' are strongly-built despatch cases covered in red, black, blue or green morocco leather and until some years ago were collected by a Palace official from the ministries in a horse-drawn maroon brougham provided by the Crown equerry from the Royal Mews. Security men, however, pointed out the vulnerability of the often highly confidential documents in this gracious old-world transport and now the boxes are collected and returned in a secure van.

Inside the boxes are a digest of the most important developments in the principal ministries. It is a constitutional right of the British monarch to be kept informed and the boxes are one of the ways of doing this. When they arrive at the Palace, the contents are sifted by the private secretary, or his deputy. The mass of paper produced by a modern government can overwhelm the minister of just one department and the Queen is supposed in theory to know what is going on throughout every department of government. Summaries and even summaries of summaries are the only way the monarch can hope to keep informed of what is really important. This is another area in which the Queen must be able to place absolute confidence in her private secretary, his deputy and assistant. It is they who in practice decide what should be put before the Queen with what comments they think are appropriate. If she reads in the newspapers or hears on radio or television an interesting item which her officials have not considered important enough to put before her – well, on their heads be it!

The boxes follow the Queen around to Windsor, Balmoral, Sandringham and even aboard the royal yacht, *Britannia*. She has developed a considerable talent in reading through documents swiftly and experience has taught her to seize on the points that matter. She devotes time to the boxes and in a period of crisis will spend hours with her officials discussing a situation.

When Sir Philip has left his office on the Privy Purse Corridor below, he goes up one floor to the Queen's room, knocks, waits for a response, enters and walks over to her desk where he greets her as 'Ma'am'. It is royal protocol for the sovereign to receive reports from her ministers and courtiers whilst they stand, but this is brushed aside when she is dealing with her principal officials and there is a lot of work to be got through as expeditiously as possible.

The private secretary and his assistants will have sifted through the mail and he will run through the important, or perhaps just interesting, letters with the Queen, pointing out what passages he thinks she might want to read. She may give an immediate decision on the reply or action to be taken and Sir Philip will take notes. She may decide to hold on to the letter and write a reply in longhand which will then be typed.

Sir Philip may then produce his key and open the red box which he has already been through. He might say, 'There are three telegrams I have left on top because you may want to read them straight away.' These telegrams would be from the Foreign and Commonwealth Office with which the monarch has close links. This is especially the case with the Commonwealth within which she is Head and Queen of seventeen monarchies and is rightly proud of her achievement in preserving and strengthening its existence. The telegrams may be news of a constitutional crisis brewing up in, perhaps, Australia, Hong Kong or Zambia. If they are not lengthy she will read them through and discuss them with Sir Philip. The matters may be of profound importance for the monarchy and the Commonwealth, and this is where Elizabeth's experience as Queen for over thirty years comes into play.

It is in the confidential interchange of views on such delicate matters that the importance of the private secretary is demonstrated. He has to be in a position by virtue of knowledge, experience and special contacts beyond the Palace to be able to consider all the implications of a situation which may affect the Crown, the country and the Commonwealth and then advise the Queen what he thinks should or should not be done. It is a daunting task, and this is why there must be a rapport between monarch and private secretary.

All is not serious, however, even in the red boxes! The regular reports of ambassadors and high commissioners in residence round the world traditionally include tales of scandal currently circulating about the rulers or prominent men and women in the countries to which they are accredited and which may, consequently, affect their standing. It could be a spicy story from Washington, Moscow, Rome or Riyadh to which the private secretary may direct the Queen's attention – without the glimmer of a smile, of course! It all helps to keep her a very well-informed woman, especially as she might later have to meet the personalities involved either here or in their own countries.

While the Queen is conferring with her private secretary it is convenient to describe him and some of his team. Philip Moore (now doubly a Knight, GCVO and KCB) was born in 1921, the son of an Indian Civil Servant of the old Raj, and was educated at Cheltenham and Oxford. Soon after war broke out in 1939 he joined the RAF and served in bomber command. He was shot down over Germany in 1942 and spent three years as a POW. At the end of the war in 1945 he went back to Oxford for a year and became a rugby and hockey blue and played cricket for Oxfordshire. He had good looks of a fairly rugged sort and by this time had become something of a latter-day John Buchan hero – highly intelligent, an excellent all-round sportsman and with a good war record. He was singled out as a 'high-flyer' by the mandarins of Whitehall and given various significant diplomatic posts around the world. Finally he was appointed Deputy High Commissioner in Singapore before being transferred to the Ministry of Defence as chief of public relations – proof indeed that public relations, not so long previously mocked and derided by the services, was important.

In Sir Philip Moore's office is Robert Fellowes, forty-one, who ranks as assistant private secretary. He is the son of the former agent of the Sandringham royal estates in Norfolk, went to Eton and did a spell with a bank in the city. Then in 1978 he married Lady Jane Spencer, who like all the Spencer girls had spent their youth in a house near Sandringham and had always been part of the scene. Three years later Prince Charles married her younger sister, Lady Diana.

Senior to Robert Fellowes is Sir William Heseltine, born 17 July 1930, an Australian, who ranks as deputy private secretary so that if Sir Philip retires in a few years it would seem likely he will succeed. Heseltine's background and career throw some light on the Queen's thinking about the future. He comes of a well-to-do family in western Australia and got a first-class honours degree in history. He was picked to join the Prime Minister's office in Canberra in 1951 and at the age of twenty-five became private secretary to Sir Robert ('Bob') Menzies who dominated the Australian political scene in the post-war years. When the Queen visited Australia in 1960 Heseltine helped with the press arrangements. By now he had developed into an Australian 'high-flyer' and in 1962 became acting official secretary to the Governor-General.

Menzies was a great Empire/Commonwealth man and won prestige as an elder statesman in its counsels. The Queen was always glad to welcome him to the Palace as a wise friend on his frequent trips to London. It was he who had suggested the six-month break in Australia during 1966 for Prince Charles at the Timbertop school camp in rugged country belonging to Geelong, the Australian Eton. The Queen was painfully aware that her son and heir had never found Gordonstoun congenial and was growing into an introverted young man. Timbertop worked magnificently. It was the changing point in Charles's development.

'Bob' Menzies in one of his talks with the Queen advised that it would be sensible for the future of the monarchy to have a few bright young people from the Commonwealth in the Palace. He mentioned his protégé, William Heseltine, whom the Queen had already seen at work. The idea was accepted and Heseltine arrived at Buckingham Palace in 1965 at the age of thirty-four and was given the job of assistant to Commander (later Sir) Richard Colville, RN, the press secretary. He had, indeed, been thrown in at the deep end!

To look back at the Palace's attitude to the press in the post-war years, it is obvious that, for a long time, it had been impervious to change. A court correspondent was officially attached there from the Press Association, the national news agency. His task was to report to the Palace and funnel out information provided by the private secretary's office. He was also given facilities to accompany royalty on certain official occasions. Generally he was a nice enough chap of reasonable background who in appearance soon became indistinguishable from other Palace officials (bowler hat, dark suit, highly polished black shoes, gloves; tweeds, trilby or cap in the country; morning coat, black or grey topper for day ceremonies; dinner jacket or tailcoat and white tie for the evening). It was, as the Army would say, 'a cushy number', but if you stepped out of line, the Palace would have swiftly asked for a replacement.

*The Times* generally had good contacts with the Palace. The Editor or one of his staff who had a suitable background would be called in and perhaps given lunch, in order that an authoritative leader would be published on a matter affecting royalty which the advisers considered should be placed before the public in the right light.

As for the rest, the Palace could depend on the loyalty of the handful of men, often ennobled, who controlled the British press. In a crisis they could always be relied on. There was, of course, in those days, Lord Beaverbrook, a loyal monarchist, but a man who went his own way and was disliked and feared by royalty.

This dyke built round the Palace to protect it from the intrusions of the press was, however, always leaking. On the 'downstairs' level, Palace servants were befriended and bribed to provide more or less factual details of life in the Palace. On the 'upstairs' level there were men, but more generally women, connected with the nobility, who were part of the social world and picked up stories at cocktail parties, dinners, race meetings, country-house visits – and, no doubt, between the sheets.

The war, however, changed social attitudes. There was as much loyalty as ever to the Crown, but the old deference and cap-touching were on their way out. Fleet Street too had changed. Annoyance at the silly amateurism of the Palace relations with the press sharpened and began to rub off on royalty itself, provoking even among the loyal papers a certain mocking tone.

So in 1947 a press secretary was appointed, responsible to the private secretary. The choice was Richard Colville, a former naval officer from a distinguished family of the nobility. But he had the most rudimentary knowledge of the press. The breakthrough in Palace relations with the press, British and foreign, was achieved, however, by a man who had always seemed in Fleet Street the epitome of the stiff-necked, pompous aristocracy – Bernard Marmaduke Fitzalan-Howard, 16th Duke of Norfolk, lay leader of the country's Roman Catholics. As hereditary Earl Marshal of England it fell upon him to organise the coronation of Queen Elizabeth II in Westminster Abbey on Tuesday, 2 June 1953. There is no doubt in my mind that the late Bernard Marmaduke Fitzalan-Howard did as much as anyone to ensure the prodigious world media success of the coronation, as well as organising superbly the ceremony itself in the Abbey.

After this, media relations generally could never again revert to the old pattern in the Palace. The young Queen and Prince Philip, who was a representative of the men who had served in the war, both soon realised the potential (for good or bad) not only of press and radio, but of the new phenomenon of television, which had, against opposition, been used in the Abbey and had made the coronation visible to the world. It was the breakthrough. The media could no longer be dismissed as a slightly disagreeable aspect of life to be given the 'tradesman's entrance' treatment. It had ironically taken a Duke to do the trick!

When he became press secretary, Richard Colville was given an office near that of the private secretary in the Privy Purse Corridor of the north wing under the royal apartments. This is indeed a corridor of power for it also contains the office of the royal money man, the Keeper of the Privy Purse who doubles as treasurer to the Queen. There are rooms for equerries, clerks, typists, footmen and even a small emergency surgery. About halfway down is a recess large enough to have on its walls the portraits of the Queen's three former private secretaries – Sir Alan Lascelles, Lord Adeane and Lord Charteris.

When Richard Colville retired in 1968 Heseltine took over as press secretary. His major achievement at this stage was to induce the

Queen, very reluctant at first, to approve the making of the television film, 'Royal Family', which was first shown a week before the Investiture of Charles as Prince of Wales in July 1969 in Caernarvon Castle. It was a joint BBC/ITV venture which had involved the Royal Family on and off for nearly a year with filming in over 150 locations. It turned out to be a major public relations triumph throughout the world and is still fascinating to watch.

The press secretary is now no longer a subsidiary official. Quite swiftly, for the Palace, he has become a man of power whose advice is often requested daily by the Queen. There was a certain inevitability that Heseltine would be promoted to his present position as deputy to Sir Philip Moore, for it was proof that the Palace realises, like governments and businesses, that this is the age of the skilled public relations man. It has been a long journey since George III appointed a court newsman at £45 pa to counter the highly unfavourable press he was receiving at the time of his attempt to put down the revolt of the American colonies.

Heseltine (now Sir William) was succeeded as press secretary by Ronald Allison, a former BBC sports reporter. He had charm and intelligence, but after a few years found Palace life somewhat stifling. He was succeeded by Michael Shea, in 1978. A Scot, educated at Gordonstoun, (like Prince Philip and his three sons), Michael Shea got a Ph.D. at Edinburgh, joined the Foreign and Commonwealth Office and was in the Cabinet Office in 1969. He is forty-five, married to a Norwegian and has written half a dozen varied books. He was Deputy Director of British Information Services in New York when the Queen paid a visit in 1976 and when Prince Charles followed suit the next year. He handled the media arrangements so efficiently in a difficult city that he was marked as a possible successor to Allison in the Palace. He is hard working, very professional and respected by the media.

One of the two assistant press secretaries is an Australian, John Dauth. The other was Mrs Anne Wall, very experienced and helpful. She is an admiral's daughter and niece of Princess Alice of Gloucester. In 1975 she married Michael Wall, assistant keeper of the Privy Purse, and recently retired from the Palace.

To give an example of Michael Shea's professional skills in public relations, consider his handling in March 1983, of the announcement that this year's Civil List (Parliament's grant to the Queen and certain members of the Royal Family) had risen only 4·7% to £4,908,000, 'by stringent economising and cost-cutting measures which are more familiar in industry'. This is due, we were told, to the watchful eyes and business acumen of Sir Peter Ashmore and Mr Peter Miles, Keeper of the Privy Purse and treasurer to the Queen.

Then the main points were hammered home – some voluntary redundancies; staff now automatically switch off unnecessary lights; they are now more likely to lunch on casseroles or cheaper cuts of meat than roast beef; used envelopes are kept for all internal mail, and first class postage permitted only when essential; substantial cuts in cleaning and stationery bills have been made; and, most significant of all, the Palace is using old newspapers for bedding in the Royal Mews as 'Shredabed'. It has been found to be cheaper, quicker to put down, and keeps the animals cleaner and warmer than straw or sawdust.

The story was so convincing that only a churlish fellow might wonder why the Civil List had not gone down by 4·7% rather than up by that amount!

Mr Peter Miles has the correct establishment background (Eton, Sandhurst, former chairman of Astley and Pearce, the money-brokers) to qualify as Keeper of the Privy Purse. He succeeded Major Sir Rennie Maudslay. His two principal aides are the deputy keeper, Major Shane Blewin (ex-Guards) and the deputy treasurer, Mr Russell Wood.

None of the jobs in this department are sinecures. The royal finances are so complicated that even expert accountants sitting on parliamentary select committees retire baffled. What is more, the subject is extremely sensitive. The Queen, normally imperturbable, can get very angry indeed when there is even the slightest criticism in Parliament or press of the finances of the Royal Family.

The Civil List has been granted by Parliament since the reign of George III in return for the surrender of most of the Crown property. In recent years it has been stressed that these allowances to the monarch and certain members of the Royal Family are not salaries, but expense accounts to cover representational duties here and abroad. There is much truth in this, but it tends to conceal that such splendid expense accounts provide a very royal standard of living.

In normal times, the Civil List was fixed at the beginning of a reign and remained unchanged. Since inflation spiralled in the late sixties, however, a financial review obviously had to be made. A fresh Civil List Act was passed in 1972 just about doubling the original sum. More inflation, however, soon made nonsense of this. Then in 1975 the Labour Prime Minister, Mr (later Sir) Harold Wilson, a staunch admirer of the Queen and monarchy, put his agile brain to work and came up with a permanent solution to the problem that delighted the

Queen and her family and satisfied Parliament and press. In an Amendment to the 1972 Act, which was approved in 1975, the annual payment was raised by around fifty per cent, but – and this was the important innovation – a Civil List estimate was to be presented each year to Parliament in the same way as all other government departments and this would result in a built-in inflation factor.

Harold Wilson had served his Queen well and when he resigned the following year, she created him a Knight of the Garter. Once a year he can be seen walking in procession with the sovereign and other members of the Order to St George's Chapel, Windsor, in his magnificent robes.

Of the total Civil List of £4,908,000 the Queen's allowance was £3,710,400 of which about sixty-seven per cent will go in salaries and wages for staff ranging from grand officials to humble cleaners. The Queen's Civil List Allowance is, however, only a comparatively small part of the State funding of the monarchy which totals around £15 million. The upkeep of Buckingham Palace, Windsor Castle, St James's Palace and Kensington Palace is defrayed by the Department of the Environment. Buckingham Palace (£2·5 million) is less costly than Windsor (£3 million). Balmoral and Sandringham are the private property of the Royal Family, but certain grants are given to cover the official expenses of the Queen when residing in her homes. All postage and telecommunications are paid for. Part of the costs incurred during State visits are refunded by the Foreign and Commonwealth Office which is also responsible for official tours abroad. The Queen's Flight (£3 million) and the royal train are also a state responsibility, but the big public expense is the royal yacht, *Britannia*, a floating palace manned by 21 officers and 258 ratings. The Ministry of Defence pays out over £3·5 million a year just in running costs.

The Queen in recent years has used *Britannia* much more as a headquarters on her visits abroad. She appreciates the privacy and quiet it can give her and also she can reciprocate entertainment.

During the Falklands conflict in 1982 the question of converting the *Britannia* to a hospital ship was raised and swiftly stifled. *Britannia* could be speedily converted, but to reconvert her would cost between £50 and £60 million.

The fact is that the royal yacht is an ageing, gracious survivor of the days when *Britannia* did rule the waves. She is magnificent to behold, inside and out, but is irreplaceable, the last of the line. The Queen has shown a certain panache in giving honeymoon trips aboard her yacht to Margaret and Snowdon, Anne and Mark Phillips, and Charles and Diana. As they say in the travel brochures, 'the trip of a lifetime'.

All these money matters involve Peter Miles and his department, but there is much more to royal finances yet. Another title he holds is 'Receiver-General of the Duchy of Lancaster'.

The Queen is Duke, yes, Duke of Lancaster and as such draws the revenues of a royal estate of 52,000 acres, now mainly in Yorkshire, but with pieces all over the country and even in London, including the land on which the Savoy Hotel stands. The Duchy lands were excluded from the George III settlement and now provide the Queen with an income of at least £600,000 a year.

As Monarch the Queen pays no income-tax nor surtax. She is not liable to capital gains tax nor is any of her property liable to estate duty. These exemptions largely account for the vast increase in the royal fortune, since this century considerable redistributive taxation has reduced, even eliminated, many great estates.

The Queen made it very clear indeed through her officials appearing before the select committee on the Civil List which examined the royal finances in 1971/72 that her private fortune is her own affair and in no way a subject for public investigation or even discussion. She did let it be known that the estimates of its size which were being bandied around – £50 – £80 – £100 million – were wild exaggerations. There is, however, a widely-held belief that the private royal fortune is, in fact, immense.

Mr Miles has to preserve order in all these labyrinthine passages through which money comes and goes. His deputy keeper with the help of the local agents looks after the private estates, Sandringham and Balmoral. The deputy treasurer administers the Civil List. The overall responsibility, however, rests with Peter Miles and includes even the finances of the Queen's racing stables – one of her favourite subjects for close scrutiny.

Fortunately, he and his deputies can count on the co-operation of Coutts, the Queen's bankers, who in recent years have built splendid new premises in the Strand near Charing Cross. The Coutts have been there a long time – Boswell wrote in his diary on 11 January 1763: 'I dined with Coutts in the Strand, my banker, a jolly, plentiful dinner with a Scotch company, and free, easy conversation.' Coutts is now part of the National Westminster Bank Group, but has remained largely independent because the royal connection brings social – and financial – rewards.

## THE BREAK-INS

The Palace break-ins by Michael Fagan on 7 June and 9 July 1982 were by no means the first.

A year after Queen Victoria moved into her new Palace (1838) the police were ordered to tighten security measures in the Palace and gardens for 'ill-looking fellows have this season frequently been seen climbing over the wall, and the sovereign's person is exposed to insult and perhaps to danger'. There were also fears in government circles that her savage uncle, the Duke of Cumberland, now King of Hanover, might have Victoria murdered for he was heir to the throne until she had a child and was considered quite capable of hiring assassins to do the work.

Two years later, in November 1840, when the Queen was lying in bed soon after the birth of her first child, Princess Victoria, a boy was found in the early hours under a settee in the room next door. He was 'the Boy Jones', who made two more unannounced visits to the Palace ('In-i-go' Jones, the wits called him after Inigo Jones, the great seventeenth-century architect) and was then given a chance to make a new life in the colonies for he was an amiable lad who meant no harm.

In the early summer of 1842 there were two serious attempts to assassinate the Queen within a few yards of the Palace and this led to improved security in the Palace. A squad of police from 'A' Division were installed to patrol the corridors all night. A plainclothes policeman was stationed at the tradesman's entrance to keep a check, but it was well-nigh impossible to have an effective surveillance of the scores of workmen and servants entering and leaving.

For example, the Queen was walking one morning through the picture gallery and saw a man apparently engaged in laying a carpet. She spoke to him and he replied in an educated voice, addressing her as 'Ma'am', not 'Your Majesty' – as a workman might. She questioned him and he confessed he was an art lover who had got in as a carpet man so that he could study the royal collection. Once more Victoria did the unexpected. She gave him permission to remain and complete his viewing!

It is even now virtually impossible to make the Palace secure during the day with painters, upholsterers, plumbers, electricians, telephone engineers and others coming and going – quite apart from a staff which is constantly changing and often reinforced by part-timers.

At night there are around eighty of the staff who sleep there and once more checking numbers and identities is just about impossible. Living-in staff, male and female, are allowed from time to time to have a friend in to spend the evening in the recreation rooms. In today's world the guest may well stay the night.

Taking this background into account, however, in no way detracts from the scandalous laxity exposed by Fagan.

Reports of intruders into the Palace gardens had become so frequent in recent years that they were something of a joke – three teenage French girls in July 1980, who had got in through a defective gate during a garden-party; three young Germans who had climbed the wall in 1981 and spent the night in the gardens believing they were in Hyde Park – to name but a couple of incidents. The police and the guards battalions were not so amused. New sophisticated detection equipment was installed and roaming sentries, not in ceremonial uniform, were on duty in the grounds during the night.

The police station in the Palace is near the Royal Mews and could not be much further away from the private apartments of the Royal Family. If you were a young, fit man and knew your way around you might, by running, make the Queen's rooms in five minutes. The police section at the time of Fagan's break-in comprised a chief inspector, an inspector, two sergeants and twenty constables, although they would not all be on duty at night.

The chain of command above the Chief Inspector, Michael Greene, was Commander Michael Trestrail, who was also in charge of the team of detectives guarding other members of the Royal Family. What is more, he had been the Queen's personal bodyguard since 1971, accompanying her on most of her engagements in Britain and her tours abroad. It was an absurd, impossible burden of very important responsibilities.

Above Trestrail came Commander Victor Lashbrook, head of 'A' District which included the Palace, Clarence House and Downing Street. His superior was Assistant Commissioner Wilf Gibson, responsible to the then Commissioner of the Metropolitan Police, Sir David McNee, and he in turn was directly responsible to the then Home Secretary, Mr William Whitelaw.

All these men were to be involved when Michael Fagan, at about 11 pm on 7 June 1982, climbed over the Palace railings in Buckingham Palace Road, shinned up a drainpipe by the ambassador's entrance, made his way across a roof or two, shinned up another drainpipe to the third floor room of a maid who saw his hand appear outside the window. She fled and told the duty policeman. Fagan, meanwhile, had got in and made his way downstairs. The policeman came to the maid's room and thought the girl must have been imagining things. Fagan roamed round the Palace looking at the pictures and decorations, found half a bottle of Californian wine in a storeroom, pushed the cork in, had a gulp or two and then got out through another window, jumped over the fence and walked away up the road.

Fagan's second visit to the Palace was at around 6 am on 9 July by the same route. He was seen climbing up a drainpipe by a policeman who was nothing to do with the Palace, but was going home on his motorcycle after night-duty. He stopped, went to the Palace police station and was more or less told to mind his own business. Fagan, meanwhile, had reached the stamp rooms on the ground floor of the Palace which lead off the Grand Hall. They contain one of the world's great stamp collections created by George V and George VI which is worth many millions. He then went up to the first floor and seems to have had a look at the Throne Room where, on the grand dais, stands the red silk and gilt chair which was made as the Queen's Chair of Estate for her coronation. Alongside is a matching throne for Prince Philip.

By now Fagan had only to cross a corridor and arrive at the Queen's apartments. Nobody was around. He opened a door, walked in, pulled open the curtains and found the Queen raising herself startled in her bed. It was an absurd event.

An armed policeman is outside her bedroom all night, but he had gone off duty. The footman had arrived, collected the corgis and taken them down to the garden for their usual morning exercise. So there was nobody to answer the bell in the lobby when the Queen pressed the button by her bedside.

Fagan was now sitting on the Queen's bed rambling on in a rather incoherent way about the problems in his life. He was not aggressive or unpleasant, but how was the Queen to know what he would do next?

He asked for a cigarette. The Queen explained she did not smoke, but would get some. She used her bedside telephone to call the police room and ask for some cigarettes to be sent, hoping they would realise something was wrong. Nothing happened. Nearly ten minutes later she rang again. Nothing happened.

Eventually the Queen's chambermaid, Liz Andrews, knocked and entered in the normal way. She saw Fagan and exclaimed in her Geordie accent: 'Bloody hell, Ma'am, what's he doing here!' The

Queen asked her to take him out and give him a cigarette. He went quietly, muttering, 'Goodbye, Your Majesty, goodbye!'

Paul Whybrew, the footman, had now arrived back with the corgis. He gave Fagan a cigarette whilst Liz dashed along the corridors to the Palace police station.

The Queen was not amused at the time the police took to arrive, especially as they went to the wrong room. Fagan was arrested. The Queen could breathe freely again. If the intruder had been a rapist or a murderer, she would have been utterly defenceless. Understandably, there was a national outcry when the news came out, followed by demands for heads to roll.

As details filtered out, the story became more and more ludicrous. The policemen at the Palace, it appeared, were either old men nearing retirement or young men studying their books for promotion examinations. Few were interested in the Palace assignment. Alarm bells that rang were generally switched off because in the past they had generally been found to be faulty or perhaps indicated a presence that was best ignored. There were enough policemen in the Palace, but they were not properly supervised. There was enough surveillance equipment, but it was not maintained or used efficiently.

As the public inquest went on there were inspired leaks that Scotland Yard had long warned Sir Peter Ashmore, Master of the Household, that the Private Apartments of the Queen and Prince Philip should be more closely guarded. It was further hinted that Sir Peter had raised the matter with the Queen and Prince Philip and that they had been distinctly cool about any increased police presence. Philip, it was added, disliked policemen plodding around the Palace corridors nearly as much as he did press photographers following him around outside.

A few, just a few, heads did roll. The unfortunate sergeant on duty outside the Queen's bedroom, Cyril Hunt, was told to resign in February 1983. He was due in any case to retire the following month after twenty-seven years service. He considered an appeal and then, perhaps, remembered the risks to his pension. Commander Lashbrook was relieved of his Palace duties, so was Chief Inspector Michael Greene. Both, however, were transferred to other jobs. No one else seems to have suffered. Sir David McNee was, in any case, retiring in the autumn of 1982. As for Mr Whitelaw, he was to prove he could survive more than the Fagan episode. In the new Government formed by Mrs Thatcher after her June 1983 election victory, he was created a Viscount and became Leader of the House of Lords.

On 19 July 1982, Mr Whitelaw announced to the House of

Commons that Commander Michael Trestrail had resigned after a confrontation with Sir David McNee in which he admitted allegations by a male prostitute of a relationship lasting years. The House was stunned, so was the nation, especially when it was revealed Trestrail had been 'positively vetted' by security officers only three months earlier. An added ironical touch was that the Queen, mindful of Trestrail's services to her over the years, had asked Mr Whitelaw if the reason for his resignation could be kept secret. Mr Whitelaw submitted to Her Majesty that this was impossible.

As for Fagan – 'I did the Queen a favour,' he had said – he spent a few months in a mental hospital in Liverpool and on release in June 1983 was in trouble again for assaulting three policemen. He was put on probation for three years.

Acting on the ancient British tradition of locking the stable door after the horse has bolted, Mr Whitelaw later announced that 138 more uniformed police officers have been assigned to guarding Buckingham Palace, St James's Palace, Kensington Palace and Windsor Castle.

## THE FUTURE

When he was in America in the autumn of 1969, Prince Philip in the course of a television appearance made some blunt remarks about the Royal Family 'going into the red'. He added, 'If nothing happens we shall have to – I don't know, we may have to move into smaller premises, who knows?'

His comments probably speeded up the review of the Civil List which inflation had made necessary. The remark about moving into smaller premises did, however, raise a point.

There, right in the middle of London, is Buckingham Palace with over 600 rooms and 350 staff and at times the question is asked, even by loyal monarchists, whether the whole organisation is not rather top-heavy for a nation now diminished in political and economic power.

In addition to these considerations, the Palace has in the past been disliked as a home by many members of the Royal Family. All houses create their own atmosphere and it would be foolish to say that the Palace gives off joyous vibrations.

The Queen, however, with Prince Philip at her side, has for over thirty years done much to banish the gloom of the past. Their four children grew up there and brought a sense of fun to the long corridors. As they became older there were many light-hearted parties with laughter and music. Anne and then Charles were married from the Palace and had their splendid wedding breakfasts there.

The Queen and Prince Philip have worked hard at their desks and performed their ceremonial duties with dignity and grace. By and large they have so organised their lives that they are not imprisoned by the Palace.

But, more important than any of these factors, is that Buckingham Palace, for all its seeming disadvantages, is for the nation, the Commonwealth and the world beyond, a potent symbol of the continuing presence of the British monarchy. To dismantle or diminish the importance of the Palace could well endanger the whole institution. On Saturday, 11 June 1983, the Queen's official birthday, she watched her Guards Trooping the Colour on Horse Guards Parade, then rode back at the head of her Household Troops. Later, with her family, she appeared on that famous balcony to greet once more her subjects waiting beyond the forecourt of

THE PALACE

# *Bibliography*

BOSWELL, James
*The Life of Samuel Johnson*, Vols I & II of Everyman's Library. J. M. Dent, 1946 edn.
*London Journal, 1762–1763*. A Signet Book by arrangement with McGraw Hill Book Co. 1956.

BROWN, Ivor
*Balmoral*. Collins, 1955.

CECIL, Lord David
*Melbourne*. Combined Edition of *The Young Melbourne* (1939), Lord M (1954) Reprint Society by arrangement with Constable, 1955.

CLARENDON, Lord (Edward Hyde)
*Selections from the History of the Rebellion & Civil Wars* etc. World's Classics, Oxford University Press, 1955.

COATS, Peter
*The Gardens of Buckingham Palace*. Michael Joseph, 1978.

FULFORD, Sir Roger
*Royal Dukes, Queen Victoria's 'Wicked Uncles'*. Pan Books, 1948.

HEDLEY, Olwen
*Buckingham Palace*. Pitkin Pictorials Ltd, 1976.

HIBBERT, Christopher
*The Court of St James's*. Weidenfeld & Nicholson, 1979.

HOWARD, Philip
*The Royal Palaces*. Hamish Hamilton, 1970.
*The British Monarchy*. Hamish Hamilton, 1977.

HUSSEY, Christopher
Introductory chapter on buildings and site to *Buckingham Palace* by H. Clifford Smith, (q.v.)

LACEY, Robert
*Majesty*. Hutchinson, 1977.

LANE, Peter
*Prince Philip*. Robert Hale, 1980.

MACAULAY, Lord (Thomas Babington)
*The History of England*. Everyman's Library, J. M. Dent.

MILLAR, Sir Oliver
*Surveyor of the Queen's Pictures since 1972.*
*Contributed when Deputy Surveyor to Buckingham Palace.*
Thomas Nelson, in conjunction with *Sunday Times*, 1968.
The introduction was by John Russell, the art critic. The architecture was described by John Harris, then Curator of Drawings at the R.I.B.A. Geoffrey de Bellaigue, then Deputy Surveyor of the Queen's Works of Art, dealt with his subject. Also by Sir Oliver Millar & others: *Catalogue Raisonné of 'Kings & Queens' Exhibition at the Queen's Gallery, Buckingham Palace, 1982–83.*

MORRAH, Dermot
*The Work of the Queen.* William Kimber, 1958.

MORROW, Ann
*The Queen.* Granada, 1983.

MUSGRAVE, Clifford
*Royal Pavilion.* Bredon & Heginbotham, 1951.

NICOLSON, Sir Harold
*Diaries & Letters (1930–1939).* Collins, 1966.

PACKARD, Jerrold M
*The Queen and her Court.* Robson Books, 1981.

PEACOCKE, Marguerite
*The Story of Buckingham Palace.* Odhams Press, 1951.

PLUMB, J. H. & Sir Huw Wheldon
*Royal Heritage.* B.B.C. 1977.

POPE-HENNESSY, James
*Queen Mary.* George Allen & Unwin, 1959.

SMITH, H. Clifford
*Buckingham Palace.* London, Country Life, 1931. New York, Charles Scribner's.

TISDALL, E. E. P.
*Restless Consort.* Stanley Paul, 1952.

VARIOUS CONTRIBUTORS
*The Queen.* Allen Lane, 1977.

WHITING, Audrey
*Family Royal.* W. H. Allen, 1982.

WORTHAM, H. E.
*The Delightful Profession. Edward VII. A Study in Kingship.* Jonathan Cape, 1931.

# *Acknowledgements*

Whilst accepting responsibility for the selection of illustrations, the Publishers wish to express their grateful thanks for the generous advice and guidance received from various sources, but in particular from: Mr Marcus Bishop of the Lord Chamberlain's Office, and the staff of the Print Room of the Royal Library, Windsor; and Mrs E. Tasiemka of the Hans Tasiemka Archives.

The illustrations, many of which have not been reproduced this century, are the result of extensive and painstaking research by Mr Peter Knight, who also commissioned the original paintings by Mr Michael Frith.

Photographs and illustrations are supplied or are reproduced by kind permission of the following:

Pages 37, 81,82, 83, 84, 86–87, 151, 156, 159, 163 by gracious permission of H.M. The Queen

Pages 74–75, 93 and endpapers, BBC Hulton Picture Library

Pages 103, 146–147, Camera Press

Pages 88–89, 95, 97, 100–101, 104, 113, 123, 124, 140, 167, 175 (and inset), London Express

Pages 132–133, London News Service/Barratts

Pages 117, 118, 119, 120, Michael Frith

Pages 16–17, 21, 44, 46, 48, 49, 51, 54–55, 56–57, 59, 60–61, 63, 64, 66–67, 68–69, 70, 71, Tasiemka Archives

Pages 106–107, W. H. Allen

# *Index*